To
Josh, Lauren and Chloe
May you be lifelong learners

In Memory of
Mark Taylor
Who showed me that it's not about the years of your life
but the life in your years

**Special Thanks to My Team
For Making This Book a Reality**

Don Draper

Eleanor Joyce

Barb Sulava

Robbie Sulava

Mike Warnell

You guys make me look good!

Acknowledgment and Apology

After printing "Still Walking", I realized that I had not included anything in the book about the people that helped make it happen. Don Draper did an excellent job with cover design. Eleanor Joyce and Barb Sulava both did fantastic work in editing my manuscript. As you saw on the previous page, they are the same group that has helped make this book happen as well.

The one person that I truly need to apologize to and give lots of credit to is my friend, **Mike Warnell**. Without his assistance, I would not have come up with the names for either of my books. The working title for "Still Walking" was so pathetic that I don't even remember what it was. His idea to call it "Still Walking" was brilliant and he has launched a whole "Still…" franchise.

Mike, you are the man and I hope that putting that in writing for all the world to see will make up for not having done it before!

Video Access

I'm delighted to make this book a full multimedia experience! As you will see, each of the chapters includes a link to a video which further reinforces the lesson from the chapter.

To access the videos, you will need to create a username at:

http://www.yourmotivationalspeaker.com/register/

The password to access this page is:

20stories+lessons

Throughout the book you will also find QR codes like the one below. If you have a smart phone or a tablet, you can use a QR reader app to scan these codes and they will take you directly to the link from that page. Scanning the code below will take you to the registration page.

Follow Rob on Social Media:

@imroboliver

Table of Contents

Introduction 13
1. Pride Goes Before the Fall… And After! 15
2. Dream Snatcher 19
3. Duquesne University 25
4. Dysreflexia 31
5. A Slip in the Shower 37
6. Hitting the Wall 43
7. "Real Problems" 47
8. John's Sneakers 51
9. My Name is Rob 55
10. I Want to Hold Your Hand 61
11. The Vacation From… 65
12. Brownies 71
13. Giving Directions 75
14. My Inadvertent Family 83
15. The Launch Ramp 87
16. "Trust Me" 93
17. My Name is… Bob?? 99
18. The Trip From… 103
19. Discrimination? Maybe Not! 113
20. Sandy the Social Worker 119
About the Author 125
Contact the Author 128

Introduction

Designing the cover for my book has never been easy for me. I have a professional graphic designer who can convert my ideas into reality with incredible ease. The problem is that I have to come up with the ideas.

I was talking to my nephew, Robbie Sulava, about my dilemma. As I complained about how much difficulty I was having in coming up with the concept for the cover, he reminded me of the cover of "Still Walking". It was the footprints on the beach that represented the journey of life. He suggested continuing that theme.

It made perfect sense, but what would it look like? It was at that point I was inspired for footprints through the snow in the wintertime. It's really a metaphor that speaks to the heart of what this book is about.

First, Winter is a time when the elements are stacked against you. We all find seasons in life when our environment is not friendly and conducive to growth. Sometimes, it's just about survival.

Second, snow and ice make it more difficult to walk our path. Not only does the snow cause us to work harder to make progress, it hides some of the underlying dangers. Under the snow are ice, rocks and holes which can cause us to stumble. In much the same way, there are times when we all experience "tough sledding". There are days when moving forward just is not easy.

Third, falling in the wintertime is truly dangerous. If we stay where we have fallen, we run the risk of frostbite, hypothermia and even death. There are three options facing us when we fall: lay there and do nothing, wait for someone else to come along or muster up our energy and get ourselves back up.

Fourth, and finally, sometimes the difficulty of our circumstances and the adverse elements can keep us from seeing the beauty of what surrounds us. Winter is a beautiful time of year but if we are focused on the cold, the ice and the danger, we can miss on the snow covered trees, the snowcapped mountains and the beauty of God's creation.

As you read the book, you will see some difficulties that come from my surroundings. You will see obstacles and you will see falls. However, that's not what I want you to ultimately see. This is not a book about how difficult my life is, it's not a book about "poor me". This is a book about the resiliency of the human spirit. It is not about the struggle, it's about getting back up and moving forward.

I may be "Still Falling" but I am also "Still Learning", "Still Living" and (like the Energizer Bunny) "Still Going".

Chapter One

Pride Goes Before the Fall…
And After!

One of the first times I remember falling out of my wheelchair was going to my brother-in-law Joe's house. They lived right next door to us. Becky was away and Joe and his wife Penny kindly invited me for dinner. Since they were right next door, I figured I would just ride over in my wheelchair.

Now, I must explain a little bit about the terrain where we live. In Pittsburgh, everything is on a hill. Even though our houses backed up against each other, I still had to go up the hill to get to the street that their house faced. Then I had to go down a little bit of a hill to get to their driveway. Oh, and their driveway was downhill as well.

Everything was going fine. I went up the hill to the top, turned right and started downhill to their house. I got to their driveway and that's when the problem started. As I started down the hill in their driveway my back wheels hit the curb and popped up in the air. Because my front wheels were already headed down the hill, the back wheels popping up in the air threw the balance of the chair completely off and the next thing I knew, the chair started to tilt forward and there was nothing I could do to stop it.

I let go of the joystick to see if the chair would stabilize itself. It kind of did! The next 15 seconds felt like they took place over about half an hour. Very slowly the chair tilted forward. I was thinking that it might come to a stop before it reached the equilibrium point and pop back down, but it didn't. It just kept slowly tilting further and further forward until it became dreadfully obvious that it was going to flip over forward. I put my hands up to brace myself as the chair launched forward. I landed face down and then rolled sideways.

Let me paint a picture for you. I am now lying in the driveway, strapped to my wheelchair which is completely on its side. There is nobody outside, just me, by myself in the driveway. The road that goes by the front of their house is not very busy but at that point, a very kind woman drove by the end of the driveway. When she saw my situation, she stopped her car in the middle of the road and rolled down the window. With a concerned look on her face, she asked me, "Can I help you?"

I have no idea what I was thinking. The obvious answer should have been, "Yes, please!" For some reason, I felt that I did not need her help. I may have been thinking about how embarrassing it would be to have a complete stranger helping me. On top of that, I didn't think she was strong enough to do anything to help me. I didn't know if anyone inside the house knew that I had fallen. For some reason, I just would not accept her help. I told her, "No, I'm okay. Thank you."

I can't figure out which is more ridiculous, me telling her that I did not need help when I obviously did, or her accepting my denial of service and driving off. That's just what she did, she said okay, rolled up her window and drove away.

As she pulled away, I looked toward the house. Through the kitchen window, I could see Joe, Penny, and my father-in-law. They must have been engaged in a very interesting conversation because it definitely kept them from looking out the window.

So there I lay, proudly independent – but alone and helpless. There was nothing I could do but think about my situation. And think I did. I thought about why I turned down the only help that was available to me at the time. I thought about what I was going to have to do to alert my family about my plight. I thought about my own stupidity and pride.

Thankfully, I did not have to embarrass myself further by yelling for help. It only took about three or four minutes for the folks in the kitchen to look out the window and see me lying in the driveway. Once that happened, they came out almost immediately and helped me get everything pulled back together. I learned a major league lesson that day. Forget about right, forget about privacy, forget about dignity, when you are in need of help, it is okay to allow others to help you. You don't have to be self-sufficient everyday, all day, your entire life

Even though I don't think that the lady driving by would have been able to help me get up, she would have at least been able to alert the family about what was going on. She could have moved things along a little bit quicker than me waiting, hoping and praying that someone in the house would see me. There are times when I need to do things independently, on my own. At those times, I don't ask for help. However, I learned the important lesson that when help is offered, don't be too proud to take it. Especially if you are lying face down in the driveway with a power wheel chair strapped to your back.

Think about this
1. What keeps you from asking for help when you need it?
2. Where do you see the balance between independence and stubborn pride?

http://www.yourmotivationalspeaker.com/still-falling-videos/video1/

Chapter Two

Dream Snatcher

When our kids were little, someone gave us a "dream catcher". The legend is that if you hang it near the kids' beds, it will catch all of the bad dreams and keep them from disturbing their sleep. We don't have a "dream catcher" in our room, what I found out that we do have is a "dream snatcher"! Let me explain.

I don't often dream. Okay, maybe I do dream more often that I realize but I don't ever seem to remember them in the morning. Every now and then, I can remember a dream but not usually. Add to that the fact that my dreams are not that exciting. They seem like a mixed up version of my experiences through the day. However, one night I did have "the dream".

This dream was perfect! At least for me it was. All five senses were firing for this one. I was sitting on the beach. Not just any beach, it was a beach in the Caribbean. The kind that you see on a postcard. The sand was white and the water clear blue, so clear that you could see the bottom. The warm tropical sun shone down on me, spreading a feeling of warmth from head to toe. Just when the sun would get too hot, a small cloud would drift in front of it to provide a few moments of shade and a chance to cool down just a little bit. A warm tropical breeze blew across the beach. It was not a cold breeze, it was not a hot wind, it was just the right temperature to add to that feeling of warmth without being oppressive. A stand of four palm trees was right behind my head. When the breeze blew, the palm fronds danced in front of the sun to provide some appreciated shade.

I was comfortable, relaxed. It was almost as if I had been here before. As I looked around, I recognized the beach, I had been here before. This was the beach on CocoCay. It was the beach that I had sat on when our family went on the cruise to celebrate Becky and my 20th wedding anniversary. One of the main differences was, this time, there were not 600 other people on the beach. The only people I could see were my wife, lying in a chaise beside me, and my three kids in their bathing suits headed towards the water carrying flippers and a mesh bag with snorkels and facemasks. The smiles on their faces went from ear to ear.

I was close enough to the water to hear the gentle waves lapping against the sand. The wind blowing through the palm trees made the sound of rustling leaves. In the distance I heard the horn of a cruise ship dropping anchor just offshore. The sound of the tropical birds flying overhead was beautiful. So different than the squawking of the seagulls that I was used to at the beaches of New Jersey. From the center of the island, the sound of reggae music drifted towards me. I heard the crunch of ice in the cooler as fresh drinks were being brought out for our family. A faint sizzle could be heard through all of the other noises.

I wondered what was sizzling, then the smell hit me. It was the smell of the grill. The smell of steak, the smell of island spices on the fish and chicken and shrimp. The delicious aroma triggered my Pavlovian instinct and the relationship between my sense of smell and my sense of taste became clear as my mouth began to water.

This was the best dream ever. I was enjoying every moment when all of the sudden, everything went black. When you are knocked unconscious, you close your eyes and everything goes black. In this particular instance, I opened my eyes and everything was black. I was no longer on the beach. I couldn't hear anything. I didn't smell anything. My mouth was no longer watering. I couldn't see anything.

I was completely disoriented. Where was I? What happened? It took a moment for things to become clearer. My senses slowly came into focus. I couldn't see anything because it was pitch dark. As my eyes adjusted, I looked around and realized that I was lying in my bed, in my bedroom, just outside of Pittsburgh Pennsylvania. It only took a second after that realization for me to feel a hand on my shoulder, shaking me. My wife's voice said softly in the darkness, "You were snoring so loud!"

Everything made a little bit more sense now. Apparently, my snoring had wakened her. Beyond that, it had kept her awake and she wanted me to do something about it. Obviously, she felt that there was some way that I was going to be able to control my own snoring.

I apologized and lay quietly in the darkness. It felt like only 30 seconds had passed before I heard her breathing slip into a quiet rhythm that indicated that she was sound asleep. I closed my eyes and figured I would join her.

But wait, what about my dream? That awesome, excellent, perfect dream? I wanted to go back there. I was hoping that this was like watching a movie. My wife had hit the pause button, now it was time to hit play and resume watching.

The problem is that I find it almost impossible to will myself to sleep. Falling asleep is something that I can do without effort, making myself go to sleep, not so much. My eyes were closed but I was not asleep. I wanted to be asleep, but I was not. The desire to sleep filled me. To sleep, to dream! To dream that perfect dream! In order to dream that dream, I was going to have to go to sleep. Go to sleep, I thought. Why can't I go to sleep?

I tried everything in my power to ease back into sleep. Counting sheep didn't work. My wife was obviously sleeping so I began to match her breathing pattern. It was slow and relaxed, but it didn't help. As a matter fact, the more I tried to sleep, the more difficult it became. The more effort I put into falling asleep the more wide-awake I felt. After a few minutes it became obvious, I wasn't going right back to sleep. On top of that, my dream was over.

I'm not sure how long I lay there awake. It could've been 15 minutes, it could've been two hours. It was just a long, long time to wish for sleep and long for my dream. Eventually, my mind slowed down, I relaxed and sleep overtook me.

When the alarm went off the next morning I opened my eyes to see the light of sunrise streaming in our windows. As I went through the events of the previous night in my mind, I realized that the time between when Becky woke me up and the alarm woke me up was just a black spot. I hadn't dreamed anything let alone returned to my wonderful dream.

For the next few weeks I searched for my dream. Every night as I got into bed I wondered, "Can I reclaim the dream tonight?" Every morning as I awoke, the answer came back to me, "No!" The dream was over. It wasn't coming back. It was gone, gone, gone forever!

It was at that point that I labeled my wife a "dream snatcher". She had (very unintentionally) killed the most beautiful and wonderful dream ever. It was gone and it was her fault.

Looking back on it, I realized that many of us have dreams and aspirations throughout our lives, not just when we are sleeping. Thoughts about what we would like to be when we grow up. Goals about what we would like to accomplish with our lives. Hopes for what we will someday be.

Sadly, circumstances often come about that alter that dream. Most of the time, it's something beyond our control. Sometimes, it's just fate that becomes our "dream snatcher".

The challenge is, what we do when our dream is taken away? Have you ever met someone who, as an adult, tells you stories about what he or she should be? Perhaps you've heard stories about a guy who is a tremendous athlete with a professional future ahead of him until he blows out his knee. Maybe it's the story about a young lady who wanted to be a writer but her English teacher just didn't "get her". I'm sure there are a myriad of other such examples.

The sad thing is that sometimes people get stuck right there. Their dreams were snatched away and they spend the rest of their lives longing for the dream. They share the stories about what they were supposed to be, what they would have accomplished and that's as far as it goes.

A few weeks after my wonderful dream, I finally gave up on reclaiming it. I have not re-dreamed it but I have had some other great dreams. I learned that when the "dream snatcher" comes along, it's okay to let go of your dream and grab a new one.

In the real world, those are the stories of success and inspiration. Stories of people who reinvent themselves. When something comes along that impacts their ability to achieve their dreams and goals, they latch onto a new dream and ride it to success. They don't close their eyes wishing for the dream they missed, they look at life with eager anticipation to see what they will dream up next.

Think about this:
1. What was your dream?
2. What kept you from reaching your dream?
3. Have you dreamt a new dream?
4. How are you pursuing that new dream?

http://www.yourmotivationalspeaker.com/still-falling-videos/video2/

Chapter Three

Duquesne University

Pittsburgh is often called the City of Bridges. That makes sense to me. The city is built on three rivers, there are an inordinate number of bridges in Pittsburgh! However, it may better be called the City of Hills. Everything in Pittsburgh is on a hill.

This may not be an actual term but I have edge-phobia. I believe that I rationalized this way: a phobia is an irrational fear and my fear of edges is not irrational at all. I fear getting too close to the edge of the bed because I can't stop myself from falling off. I have a fear of getting too close to the edge of the sidewalk and my wheelchair sliding off. I think of it more as a healthy respect and less as an irrational fear. Apart from my edge-phobia, I don't think I am afraid of much of anything. The hills of Pittsburgh do make me go slowly sometimes, not only when I'm going uphill but when I'm going across the hill. However, it isn't anything that would stop me from going out.

I remember my first time going onto the campus at Duquesne University. I had been accepted for the Masters program in Psychology. To say that the campus of Duquesne is on a hill is a major understatement. It's on a cliff. I'm not kidding. At the top of the campus there is a lookout that is called the Bluff. The rest of the campus as it descends down to Forbes Avenue is steep enough that I don't believe you could just walk straight up. It's one of those places where a building is built into the hill. You can go into the front of the building on the first floor, take an elevator up to the 12th floor and go out the back of the building onto level ground.

As with most college campuses, parking is scarce at Duquesne. There were only a handful of van accessible parking places on campus and they were not always available. As a result, I had to go on a scouting excursion to find a spot that would work. That involved driving around campus, up and down hills, searching for somewhere, anywhere, that I could park, have room to put my lift out and be assured that no one would park beside me.

The van accessible spots were usually in a relatively flat area, on roads that go across the hill instead of up and down the hill. Most of the other parking was on the side streets that went straight downhill. When my scouting missions were successful, that's where I usually had to park, headed straight downhill.

It was early September and I was scouting a parking place. This particular day was sunny and beautiful. The parking situation, not so beautiful. I drove around campus for about 10 minutes before I finally found an open spot on a side street. It was a one-way street going downhill. What was unusual was it had parking on the left side of the road. That was great for me, it meant that I could easily open my lift into the middle of the road with room to spare. It also meant that no one would be able to park beside me. It did provide a great challenge because I had to parallel park. My parallel parking skills are pretty good but the fact that I was on a 45 degree angle added a significant challenge.

I nailed it on my first attempt. I was extremely proud of myself. I know that pride is not a good thing but I couldn't help myself. I also know that most of the things that I am proud of myself for are kind of goofy. This day I was proud up myself for my parking job. In one move I had backed myself into the spot perfectly. My tires were both six inches from the curb. My van was perfectly centered between the vehicle in front of me and the vehicle behind me. The crowning achievement was that there was just enough space in front of me to be able to pull out on the spot without having to back up or hit the car in front of me. It was an awesome park job!

Once I stopped admiring my parking skills (which took only about three seconds) I was faced with the daunting task of getting out of my vehicle. Getting out of the van when the lift is facing downhill is scary, getting out of vehicle when the lift is facing uphill is difficult. Getting out of the vehicle when the lift is crossways on the hill is a different matter altogether!

In spite of all that, I didn't come to campus just to arrive at campus. I didn't park in the spot just to admire my own parking skills. I was there for class. It was time to get out of the vehicle and I did just that.

One thing that I had not counted on is that if I get out of the vehicle in the middle of a block, there are no curb cuts close by to allow me to get back onto the sidewalk. I had to wait until I reached the corner of the block. Once I was safely out of my van, I closed everything up and headed off up the middle of the street to go to class.

I have no particular recollections about class that day. As you can imagine, by the time that you get into graduate school, classes all start to run together. Once class was finished, I was on my way back to the van.

Knowing that I was parked in the middle of a block, I made the decision to return to the van by street instead of sidewalk. It was the right thing to do but the results were not what I was expecting

I should probably put an aside in here about how I drive my wheelchair. I always drive with the speed turned up as high as it will go. My thought is that if the wheel chair can go fast, why wouldn't you make it go fast? I'm not going to quite go as far as Top Gun to say, "I feel the need, the need for speed!" Let's just say that I don't like to go slow.

So, let me set the scene for you. I am buzzing along at top speed down the middle of the road, about a block and a half from my van. I'm not sure what made the bump in the road, a manhole cover, a crack, a wrinkle in the asphalt or something else. When I went over the bump, my front tires bumped but my back tires jumped. The next thing I knew, my back tires had left the ground and were trying to pass my front tires. Unfortunately for me, they were successful. My wheelchair lurched forward and I fell, face first in the middle of the road.

At that point, I developed a deep sense of worry. I don't know anyone else on campus. I don't have any way of getting myself up. I have no idea what the traffic flow is on this road but I am lying in the middle of it and whatever traffic is coming is either going to have to go over me or around me.

Before my mind go through all of the nightmare scenarios that could happen as I lay in the middle of the street, my wheelchair was surrounded by five students. They didn't ask, "Do you need help?" They asked, "How do we fix you?" In other circumstances I might have (wrongly!) been offended by this question. Thankfully, I had learned enough from my experience in Chapter One to just be grateful that somebody wanted to help me.

It only took a minute or two for them to set my wheelchair back on all four wheels. My chest strap held me in the chair so once it was upright, I was as well. Of course, I had slid down to the point of almost sliding out of the chair. Even though they were able to help me quickly, we were still in the middle of the street blocking everything. Several students blocked the traffic while the others got me situated properly.

Two of the guys helped me get re-seated, one on each side. Each grabbed under my armpit and pulled up. That slid my body back into a proper sitting position in the chair and I was good to go. I thanked them all profusely! I was amazed at how gracious they were. There was a chorus of kindness. "You're welcome." "No problem." "Do you need anything else?" "Are you good from here?" There wasn't really anything else I needed so I headed off to my van.

It wasn't until I actually got in the van and was ready to drive that I realized just how dangerous that whole experience was. I could have been seriously injured as the wheelchair tipped over. The students that helped could have been elsewhere on campus. Traffic could have been moving. I took a deep breath, thanked the Lord for being safe and headed home.

The lesson I learned is that everything we do has risk. I could not let the fear of tipping my wheelchair over keep me at home though. If I was going to have any community involvement, do anything outside of my home, be a part of the world, there was a certain element of risk.

It's the same for everybody. There are bad things that could happen every single day: Car accidents, poisoning, choking, the list is endless. If we are focused on the bad things that might happen, we miss out on the good things that do.

It wasn't until I got home that the extent of my experience hit home. The look on Becky's face when I came in the door was incredible. "What happened to you?" she asked. I told her about my experiences and then asked how she knew.

Apparently, I was not quite unscathed. There was a brush burn on my cheek, one on my elbow and my shirt was completely untucked from when they pulled me up in my chair. When I was getting ready for my shower that evening we found that both of my knees were bruised.

The second lesson in this experience is that we are all more affected by our experiences than we may initially realize. Sometimes others see the impact before we do. Everything that happens to us leaves bumps, bruises and cuts. Many heal without a trace, some leave scars. I carry scars from my past experiences, they're part of the path that brought me to where I am today.

As my bruises and cuts slowly healed, I noticed that my wheelchair driving changed a little bit. It was still full speed ahead but there was an increased awareness of the bumps that lay ahead and a slight slow down to go over them. Although I couldn't feel the bruised knees, I didn't want to have a repeat performance. If we're willing to learn, experience is the best teacher.

Think about this:
1. What scars do you carry from your past?
2. What lessons have you learned?

http://www.yourmotivationalspeaker.com/still-falling-videos/video3/

Chapter Four

Dysreflexia

One of the most dangerous side effects of a spinal cord injury, at least a highlevel injury like mine, is autonomic dysreflexia. What is that you ask? Well, I'm going to channel my inner middle school English teacher. Autonomic means that it has to do with the nervous system. Dysreflexia breaks into two root words. The first one is "dis", meaning not. The other word is "reflex". So just like the opposite of orderly is disorderly, the opposite of properly functioning reflexes is dysreflexia.

Now that you have the definition, I suppose you want me to explain how it works (or doesn't work.) Not a problem. For example, I don't sweat when it's hot and I don't shiver when it's cold. That creates an issue when I am outside in the summertime, I don't have any automatic way to cool down. It sounds nice, no sweat, less body odor, nothing dripping in your eyes, all definite pluses. That being said, overheating becomes a problem. The solution is a spray bottle full of water when I'm enjoying the summer sunshine and my internal body temperature rises.

Notice that I didn't say that I don't sweat at all. I do. Just for really odd reasons. For example, when my bladder gets overfilled, I break out in a sweat. Not just any old sweat, a cold, clammy, dripping sweat. This is especially an issue during the wintertime. It's freezing outside and I am dripping cold sweat. My shirt and sweater end up soaked and there's no way to dry them out easily. I'm usually cold anyway but the only solution I have is to get in the van and put the heat on as hot as it can go, fan on high and coming out the vents instead of the floor boards. Why the vents?

I can only feel the heat if it's blowing on my upper body and face. Plus, it helps dry out the cold, wet collar of my shirt.

One of the other manifestations of autonomic dysreflexia has to do with my blood pressure. When something is wrong with me physically, my blood pressure skyrockets.

When something is wrong below the level of my injury, the message goes racing up the spinal cord to the point of the break and stops. It doesn't get to the brain. Without a spinal cord injury, the message gets to the brain and is handled subconsciously. Once the brain receives the message and processes where pain or discomfort is originating, it can send a message to calm down the body and relax the muscles. The problem for me is that since the message doesn't get to the brain, there is no response to relax the body. My body continues to to ramp up for something to happen, the "Fight or Flight" concept, but my brain isn't giving a response because it never got the message. Depending on how things go, my blood pressure (which usually runs on the low side, really low, like 85/60) quickly escalates. There are times when it had been higher than 200/140. The imminent danger of this high blood pressure is a risk of stroke or heart attack. Stroke is one of my major fears. I have enough physical complications going on as it is, I don't need a stroke to further lessen my physical abilities or affect my cognitive abilities.

Believe it or not, there is a good reason that I explained all of this information. It goes back to when I originally moved to Pittsburgh. I had to find a new rehabilitation doctor, a new neurologist, a new urologist and who knows what all else. My rehab doctor was great. He had studied at Magee where I did my rehab and we were pretty much on the same page. I say pretty much, not because of a disagreement, but because of one of his referrals, the referral to a new urologist.

The urologist and I did not hit it off from our initial meeting. Mostly because he didn't listen to me at all. I explained to the urologist exactly how we were managing my bladder. We had only been doing this for two years so when he told me that he thought there was a better way to handle things, I figured he is the doctor, he has a medical degree, I should listen. I wasn't having any problems, I was just open to doing things in a new and "better" way.

That was a mistake. I had two years of experience in dealing with a spinal cord injury. He had years of medical school and practice experience dealing with patients' bladders but I don't think he had dealt with spinal cord patients before.

Following the doctor's orders, we changed up my bladder management program. He put me on medication that would relax my bladder and allow it to hold more urine. I had told him that I did not like that concept. What he was proposing was exactly the opposite of what I've been told rehab. The system had been working just fine for two years so I was comfortable with continuing the current plan. He insisted, so I went along with him.

I started on the new medication. At that point in our lives, I was still in school and Becky was working night turn. She would leave for work around 10:30 at night and come home around 7:30 in the morning. I missed her but I could usually sleep through my loneliness. The plan was that I had an attendant help me get in bed at night and then Becky would get me up and dressed in the morning before she went to bed. This was before cell phones were everywhere. In order to be safe, I did keep the cordless phone in bed with me so I could call someone if there was a problem.

It took less than a week of the new medication before we had a problem. I didn't usually wake up until Becky came in the door and I heard the noise of her moving around the house. It was a little weird when I woke up one morning just before she got home.

The next day I was awake for 20 minutes before she got home. It didn't take more than few days before I was awake a full hour and a half before she was arriving home. Being awake was one thing but before long, I had a pounding headache to go with being awake. It was only a little while before I realized what was happening. The medication was doing what it was supposed to, it was relaxing my bladder to allow it to hold more. The unintended side effect was that my bladder capacity had not raised. Holding more in was causing discomfort to the bladder and my body could not handle the higher volume.

It finally progressed to the point that I was waking up about two hours before she got home, with a pounding headache. My fears about my elevated blood pressure and the risk of a stroke ran through my mind as I lay in bed by myself. The pounding was so intense one morning that I did the only thing I could think. I called Becky at work and asked her to come home and help. She was not done her shift but made arrangements to get out a little bit early so she could come help me. The next morning, it was even earlier and the pounding was more intense. Not knowing what else to do, I called her again.

This time, she was only able to get out of work about 15 minutes early. I lay in bed, miserable with my pounding head, worried about what the consequences might be and feeling terribly alone. Time slowed to an absolute crawl. Every time I checked the clock, it was only a minute or so since the last time I'd looked. Waiting was brutal. With my eyes closed, I breathed slowly in and out, trying to be calm. My head continued to ache with no relief. Sleep was not an option. If I could fall asleep, time would move faster but the headache kept me awake.

Finally, Becky arrived home and in just a few moments she helped drain my bladder. My blood pressure returned to normal and the pounding quickly dissipated and in under two minutes it was gone. We talked about what was going on. If Becky was going to keep her job, she could not continue this trend of having to leave early every day. It was getting worse, especially since it was getting earlier and earlier that she had to leave. Eventually, we decided to abandon the new medication, go back to what we had been doing previously and see what happened. Just that quickly, the problems with waking up and having headaches went away. We returned to the "old way" of bladder management without incident.

One lesson that I learned was to trust my instincts. In communicating with medical professionals, I was responsible to ensure that my doctors understood my perspective and be certain that we were on the same page moving forward, even if it meant disagreeing with them. The more important lesson that I learned is risk is everywhere! Here I was, lying alone, doing absolutely nothing except lying in my bed and I was running the risk of heart attack, stroke and further impairment.

I know that the world is full of danger. Leaving your house in the morning puts you at risk! My experience with dysreflexia showed me that I didn't have to leave the house… I didn't even have to get out of bed to be in danger. It made me realize that there was nowhere to hide from risk. It's there, if you live in fear of what might happen you don't go anywhere. If you don't go anywhere, you never know what might happen when you're engaging the community and then the world. So go out, live life, take risks and make great things happen!

Think about this:
1. What do you fear?
2. What are your fears keeping you from achieving?

http://www.yourmotivationalspeaker.com/still-falling-videos/video4/

Chapter Five

A Slip in the Shower

It goes without saying that I need a lot of help. I do as much as I can for myself but there are just some things that I cannot do. The argument can be made that I need a lot of help between my ears, but I'm leaving that one alone.

The two major times that I need assistance are getting up in the morning and going to bed at night. Nighttime is a bit more intense, it involves getting a shower, not just getting in bed. One of the people that helps me in the evening is my friend Ron.

It is no understatement to say that Ron is meticulous. His car is spotless. When he wears a necktie you can bet that it has a little dimple right in the middle of the knot. Ron's day job is at a car dealership. His meticulous nature shows up there as well, ensuring that cars that are on the lot for sale have been thoroughly detailed and clean.

When it comes to helping me, Ron is just as detail oriented. There are times when I feel like I am a car getting cleaned. Every nook, every cranny, every everything gets thoroughly scrubbed.

I'm not complaining! If it was the opposite, that would be bad. All I'm saying is that when Ron helps me, I don't have to worry about him missing a single spot.

This is a little embarrassing to admit in a book that is being distributed worldwide, but every now and then my body functions are not 100% regulated. This story is about one particular night when there was a problem with my catheter and I ended up with a leak.

Ron was discrete about it. We had developed a code to be able to discuss things without making it completely and totally embarrassing. I just told him that it was "Yellow Tuesday" and he knew what I was talking about. This is a compliment to Ron that I'm not sure if he really appreciates. If there were anyone that I want to help me on this kind of day, Ron is that guy. His scrubbing makes sure that there are no leftovers smells of any variety and everything is squeaky clean.

It might help at this point to explain the shower procedure. The power wheelchair I use to get around is battery-operated and cannot go into the shower. I have another wheelchair that is designed specifically for the shower. It has a metal frame with a waterproof coating. Our home has a "roll-in" shower. The bathroom has tile floors, walls and ceiling. There is a shower hose mounted on the wall and a drain in the middle of the floor.

There is a process to follow to get undressed as well as move from the power wheelchair to the shower chair. Sitting in my power chair, I take off my shirt and then transfer into bed to finish getting undressed. Once that happens, I am transferred into my shower chair and can roll right into the bathroom.

Because of the extenuating circumstances of Yellow Tuesday, Ron redoubled his usual scrub. He starts with getting an appropriate lather covering every square in of the wash cloth before he even starts to scrub. Once he had washed everything, he rinsed off the soap. Now that was a thorough job, but not quite up to his standards. No, in order to replace any bad odors that may have been missed during his initial wash, he would re-scrub with something that had a little bit nicer smell, usually it was body wash.

The first step was to rinse all the soap from the wash cloth. Then the procedure was the same, pour body wash on the cloth, work up a full lather covering the entire cloth and do the re-scrub. Of course, body wash not only smells nicer that a bar of soap it also gives much better suds which gives Ron a sense of satisfaction.

This night, once he was done the re-scrub, he stood up with his face scrunched in thought. I didn't know exactly what was coming but I figured there was something that did not meet his satisfaction.

Sure enough, he was worried about the underside of my legs. Because I was sitting in the shower chair, they were in contact with the seat and he had not been able to scrub them. He was not going to be satisfied until everything was clean. That included the underside of my thighs.

He added a little bit more body wash to the cloth and picked up my left leg to scrub underneath it. Once it was cleaned and met his specifications, he put it back down and picked up my right leg.

One of the things that he had not contemplated in this whole experience is what happens when you cross human skin, soap, warm water, and a rubber seat. We learned pretty quickly, it turns more slippery than a wet banana peel. It only took one second for this fact to play out. Before I could blink or say anything my backside slid right off the seat and straight onto the floor.

With tile covering every surface of the room, I was worried about hitting the floor, having the chair shoot out from behind me and smashing my head on the floor. Thankfully, that didn't happen. I was still strapped to the chair. The strap around my chest that kept me sitting upright in the chair did exactly what it was supposed to do. It held me in. With my backside sliding off the chair onto the floor, the wheelchair had kicked out behind me and the strap slid up my chest as far as it would go becoming firmly tucked under my armpits. The pressure of the strap pulled my arms up in the air. As an additional issue we were unaware of, I was not just sitting on the floor, I was actually sitting on the drain.

Panic set in! We should have turned off the water but that wasn't even on our radar. The water was running but it had nowhere to go. It began to form a puddle, actually, it began to form more of a lake around me.

It happened that Becky's sister and her family were living with us. Becky's brother-in-law Michael is one of the strongest people I know and I think that Ron figured the only thing to do was get Michael to help us.

The name Mike only has one syllable but when Ron was hollering, that one syllable took about 20 seconds to come out! As Ron was hollering, he ran out of the bathroom, through the bedroom and in to the living room where Mike was watching TV. Sitting in the bathroom alone, I had no idea what was said between the two of them but I do know that they didn't just walk back, they ran back into the room. Michael's eyes were about the size of saucers when he saw me. They undid the chest strap, righted the shower chair and then they looked at me. Here I was, sitting on the floor. What are we going to do now?

Their instinct was to grab me by my arms and drag me up into the chair. I, on the other hand, didn't want my arms to be pulled from the sockets. We finally decided that one of them would grab around my chest, the other would grab my legs then they would pick me up and place me back into the shower wheelchair. Thankfully, the soap had washed off while I was sitting in the middle of my miniature lake.

There were a number of things that I learned that night. The important one is the difference between the "perfect world" and the "real world". In a perfect world, every single square inch of me could be scrubbed, cleaned and rinsed. In the real world, we need to wash everything possible but make sure that I stay in the wheelchair.

This lesson comes into play over and over again. During the winter in a perfect world, I would have a heated cleaning device in my garage that would allow me to come in from the snow and ice and have my tires automatically thawed and cleaned. In the real world, I come into the house with my tires packed with snow and ice and sit on an old towel waiting for the tires to defrost.

The perfect world is a theoretical, imaginary place. It doesn't really exist! There are things that would be nice about that perfect world but we live in the real world. I am firmly entrenched on "planet reality". It is my choice to focus on what could happen in the imaginary perfect world or to make the best of my situation here in the real world.

Think about this:
1. How do you balance "perfect world" vs. "real world"?
2. What is the difference between high standards and perfectionism?

http://www.yourmotivationalspeaker.com/still-falling-videos/video5/

Chapter Six

Hitting the Wall

Even though I classify myself as an expert wheelchair pilot, it seems like every so often my driving skills take a nosedive. Most of the time, I am able to safely navigate through openings with very little clearance on either side. Then, almost overnight, I begin to brush up against doorways, run into walls, bump into corners and hit the edges of the furniture.

You would think that twenty years of driving a wheelchair would give you a good sense of judging distances. I have had the same model of wheelchair since I left rehab. It can't be a lack of familiarity with the equipment. It obviously cannot be a problem with me. The first time it happened, I had to think the whole process through before I finally came up with a solution. Thankfully, I came up with the answer before I left my mark on all of the walls, tables and doorways in our home.

About six months before our wedding, I got my first power wheelchair. It was awesome! It gave me enormous freedom. About three months after our wedding, we moved into our own home. It was custom-built and designed to be both accessible and beautiful.

When things started to get messed up with my wheelchair, tire scuffs began appearing on the freshly painted walls announcing, "Rob was here." Becky would remind me that I needed to be careful. She did not want the house all marked up with tire marks. In my mind, I was being careful, I was not sure what the problem was but it was definitely not my driving skill! There had to be some reasonable explanation for the change.

My first theory was that someone had moved the furniture. One of the things that I was consistently brushing up against was the couch in the living room. I figured that the couch must move a little bit every time someone sits down. After a few months of people sitting on it, it would have moved a lot. We moved the couch back to its original position but it still did not fix the problem because now I was bumping into the edge of the kitchen counter and that definitely had not moved. I was going to have to come up with a new theory.

Theory number two was that it was a cushion problem. The cushion that I sit on is filled with air and the pressure inside can be adjusted to provide an even distribution of my weight and make sure that I do not develop any bedsores. If the cushion was losing air, that would definitely change my perspective. It seemed like a fairly reasonable guess. The good news was, it had a simple solution. We checked the cushion. It was a little bit low so we added some air pressure.

The additional air pressure helped me sit up a little bit. It did give me a little bit of height, but it did not stop me from bumping into things. Before long, I realized that the problem was not a height thing, it was a side to side thing.

Becky also had a theory. She felt that I might need to go back to rehab and get some "driving lessons" for my power wheelchair. I did not subscribe to her theory at all! I had only been out of the hospital for about a year, I was not going back! Besides that, I knew two things. First, I was being extra careful and super safe. Second, I'm a good driver!

For about four weeks, I went around being extra cautious when I came to narrow places. The weird thing was that even though I was being careful, I still was cutting it very close on one side. For the life of me I could not figure out why everything seemed to be a little bit skewed.

It wasn't until one of my friends asked me if I was sitting properly in my chair. He said that I looked crooked. I felt fine. When we looked at how I was positioned in the seat, I was sitting perfectly square. He took a step back, looked at me and said that I still looked crooked. It was then that we realized that the seat of the wheelchair was slightly twisted on the base. It was only a couple of degrees off-center, but it was enough to make a big difference.

Imagine if your face and your hips were out of line by five degrees. Instead of your body walking where you were looking, it veered off five degrees to the left. You would be running into things just like I did.

I'm not sure how long it took to get off by that much, but it explained why my judgments were off. It took a little bit of effort, but my friend was able to help me turn the seat of the wheelchair. Now, my line of sight and my line of drive were together.

The seat of the chair being off-center took place gradually and slowly. In much the same way, our perspective on our lives and ourselves can gradually slip out of line with reality.

Now, when I start to bump into things, I know how to fix the problem. The lesson is pretty simple, if your perspective is off, your judgment is impaired. A small change in perspective can create major change in the judgments that you make.

Think about this:
1. How does your perspective frame your understanding?
2. How would your judgment be changed if you took time to look at things from a different perspective?

http://www.yourmotivationalspeaker.com/still-falling-videos/video6/

Chapter Seven

"Real Problems"

One of the problems I faced early on in my speaking career was finding places to speak. There weren't very many organizations that knew who I was. Even fewer were aware of the fact that I was a speaker. The list of groups that were willing to pay me to speak was very short! In order to get my name out there, I started with speaking engagements (pro bono of course) for local service organizations such as the Rotary Club, Lions Club and Kiwanis. In addition to being a good place to gain publicity and improve my speaking skills, it also provided an opportunity to sell my newly printed book, "Still Walking".

My presentations at the service clubs were based on things that I had written about in "Still Walking". My experiences had taught me so much and I wanted others to benefit from them. You don't get much more practical and insightful into what it means to be a human being than sharing your own personal life story.

It was a great experience. I got to meet a number of wonderful people. A side benefit for me was that the people I was meeting were active members of the community and helped make connections to other organizations and businesses that might be interested in having me do a program for them. It was a privilege to support organizations that are dedicated to community service. My presentation was usually at the end of the meeting so I got to sit through the "business part" of their meetings and listen to the activities that the clubs were involved in and the services that they provided. I was always impressed with the dedication to the community that each of the clubs displayed. After my presentation, I had a chance to evaluate my marketing ability by seeing how many books I sold. I can safely say that I sold enough books at each presentation to at least cover the amount of gas that I used getting to and from the location. (If you consider that I drive a full-size van which only gets about 12 miles to the gallon, you understand that that is saying something!) The other nice thing is that I got a free meal for my effort.

I was really enjoying doing these presentations. The feedback had been really good and book sales were solid. It seemed like I was developing a good rapport with the audiences. People were coming up to me while I was selling and signing books to tell me which part of my message resonated with them.

It was after about the 10th program that I met a gentleman whose feedback changed my whole perspective on what I was doing. He was an elderly gentleman, with a soft face and warm smile. He had purchased the book and as I was signing it we started to talk. He explained, "I really appreciated your presentation today." I told him I was glad to hear that. It was then that he said, "Yeah, I used to think that I had big problems in my life, but then I listened to your presentation. The fact is, you have real problems!"

I wasn't quite sure what to think about what he said. At first, I was complemented. I was gladly taking in his first statement. I was so happy because he told me that he appreciated my presentation. I felt like Sally Fields at the Oscars, "They like me, they really like me!" I handed him his signed book and smiled as he walked away.

It was then that the impact of his second statement hit me. Wait, what did he mean by the fact that I have "real problems". I didn't come there and speak so that people would feel sad for me. My presentation was not intended to make people feel guilty for complaining about their problems. It wasn't a problem comparison at all.

I admit, some of my limitations are obvious just by looking at me. My purpose was not to put other people's problems in perspective by comparing them to my own. It was not my intention to show people how bad my limitations were and then light a fire under them by telling them that if I can succeed in spite of all of these limitations, then you can succeed in spite of what little limitations you face.

The important challenge I faced that day was to be absolutely certain of what I was communicating. The question became, "What do I want my audience to do with the information that I give them?" Strangely enough, the gentleman's statement helped clarify exactly what I was trying to say to my audience.

My message was not about my problems versus your problems. It's about the fact that everybody has problems. Limitations are part of the human condition. We all have strengths, we all have weaknesses. Everybody is faced with obstacles, both internal and external. What we have is the potential to overcome those obstacles, to thrive in the midst of difficult circumstances.

Additionally, my message was not about me being a hero or about me being inspirational. My stories were simply there to share how I have learned to enjoy life. It's not about putting me up on a pedestal as someone who has overcome such tremendous obstacles. It's about understanding that we all have issues. I have mine, you have yours. It's likely that I couldn't deal with your situation any more than you could deal with mine.

The lesson is this, I am not living to inspire others. People with disabilities aren't inspirational. Limitations are a naturally occurring part the "human condition". Everyone has problems! Everybody experiences limitations. Dealing with these limitations gets to the essential heart of what it means to be human. No matter the circumstances, no matter the limitations, it's about freedom, independence, self worth and relationships.

Think about this:
1. What are the limitations in your life?
2. What are your strengths?
3. How can you use your strengths to be more engaged?

http://www.yourmotivationalspeaker.com/still-falling-videos/video7/

Chapter Eight

John's Sneakers

Facebook has opened a tremendous opportunity to connect with people worldwide. In addition to my friends and family around the country and around the world, I was able to reconnect with some of my school friends from elementary, junior high, and high school. One of the conversation threads centered on a shoe store that was in the neighborhood called "John's Shoes". Just the mention of the name brought back a flood of memories.

"John's Shoes" was our local source for inexpensive sneakers. That's all they carried, sneakers. The store was small. It didn't have any displays, all it had were homemade metal racks against the wall. The racks were about 12 inches deep and consisted of a series of metal shelves from floor to ceiling with a metal strip running vertically every three feet. Between the strips, each of the shelves had a sticker with a handwritten number on it indicating what size sneakers were on that shelf. Stuffed in between the shelves were pairs of sneakers in clear plastic bags with their size written on the rubber at the heel in black marker. At John's, you didn't get a box, you didn't get extra laces, you didn't get anything but a pair of sneakers in a bag at a discounted price.

The shelves were painted gray, the walls were painted gray, the carpet was a bluish gray. There were three or four picnic benches in the store where you could sit down to try on shoes. Usually, the store was crowded enough that you had to sit on the floor while you were trying on shoes because the benches were all taken. There were a few stepladders scattered around so you could reach the higher shelves. There was only one cash register. It was right by the door and the old man we called John stood behind it.

There were three things that stood out to me about John's. First, the smell of new shoes. Even though it was a small hole in the wall shop with a dingy interior, that smell of new leather, glue and who knows what else defined the place. The second thing about John's was the telephone wire in front of the shop. I don't know if this is just a Philadelphia thing or if this happens in other cities as well. After kids got their new shoes, they would take their old shoes, tie the shoelaces together and throw them over the wires running between the telephone poles across the street. Every time we went to John's, there seemed to be about a dozen pairs of shoes hanging off the wires. I always begged my mom to let me throw my shoes up there, but much to my disappointment she never let me. The third thing that really stood out to me was the stigma of shopping there. John's had a lot of sneakers but they never had the really cool kind. They never had brands like Nike. Instead, they had brands like Pony and Converse. Of course, the first thing you had to do when you brought home a new pair of shoes from John's was try to erase where the size had been written. The kids in school that had money showed up in their nice new Nike sneakers. Those of us that could not afford the latest styles showed up in our Pony sneakers with gray smudges on the heel. As good as it was to have new sneakers, you were still a little embarrassed because everybody knew that you got them at John's.

In the middle of my reminiscing, I became acutely aware of the power of labels. I was worried about the brand label on the shoe. If it didn't say Nike, it wasn't cool. The gray smudged heels also were a label. It said that we didn't pay full price for the lesser brand shoes.

I was amazed as I read the Facebook comments to learn just how many other people got their shoes from John's. As a kid, I was pretty sure that I was the only one dealing with this embarrassment. It wasn't until my Facebook connections filled in the rest of the story that I realized that I was not alone.

Labels are a major issue for people with disabilities as well. It is incredible to understand the stigma associated with disability. In much the same way as shopping at John's meant that you were not one of the "cool kids", having a disability can make you feel like you are anything but "normal". A compounding issue is also that feeling of aloneness. There are times when I feel overwhelmed with my situation and I feel as though nobody truly understands what I go through.

As embarrassing as it may have been to wear sneakers from John's, once we started to play on the playground it didn't matter. When I dribbled the ball up the court, nobody said, "Hey, kid with shoes from John's, pass the ball over here!" Once the game started, my ability to play spoke for itself. Sometimes, the kids with the cool shoes were not that good at playing. Sometimes, the kids with the Ponys on played pretty well. It wasn't about the shoes, it wasn't about the labels, it wasn't about where you bought them. It was about how you played!

That's what I'm looking for in life, the opportunity to show what I can do. Sometimes, it feels like people with disabilities are not being picked for the team or if they are on the team, they are sitting on the bench. If they were able to get into the game, it would provide an opportunity for them to demonstrate to their teammates just what they are capable of.

In my ideal world, everyone would be judged on how they perform rather than any other criteria. It's not about your disability, it's not about your nationality, it's not about your age, it's not about how you dress, it's about who you are and what your strengths are. Without the opportunity to demonstrate that, it might be easy to believe that you don't deserve to be on the team.

Think about this:
1. How do you "get in the game" to show what you can do?
2. Who can you help "get off the bench"?

http://www.yourmotivationalspeaker.com/still-falling-videos/video8/

Chapter Nine

My Name Is Rob!

A lot of effort is being put into changing the way we speak. Calling someone "retarded" evokes a label with loads of baggage. Now there's effort to eliminate the use of the "R Word". To change the thought process related to people with disabilities, there's a movement towards "Person First" Language.

In order to truly understand the evolution to "Person First Language" you have to look at the history of how people with disabilities have been talked about. Legend has it that back in 1504, England was involved in a long and bloody war. As a result of the war, many of the soldiers had physical disabilities. Many were missing limbs as the result of wounds received during battle. As a result of the poor medical attention being given to the soldiers in battle, there were a number of the returning soldiers that had complications because of improperly healed broken bones. In addition to all that, infections were rampant. One of the battle tactics was use of a sword that was not cleaned. When soldiers were on parade, swords were to be shiny and polished to create an intimidating appearance. On the battlefield, it was a different story. Anything that got on the blade would stay: blood, dirt, body fluids, and so on. That way, bacteria built up along the blade and when a wound was inflicted on the enemy, that bacteria was delivered immediately into the open wound. It was highly likely that the wound would become infected with the introduction of those germs. As a result, the healing process would take longer and without a whole lot of medical options, more soldiers died from infection than from actual wounds.

After the war, King Henry VII took pity on all of the soldiers that had disabilities. He decided that it was highly unlikely that any of them would be able to go back to their former work. There were no other jobs that the soldiers would be able to perform. He reached the conclusion that these soldiers would not be able to contribute anything to society. In 1504, it was against the law to beg. As a display of appreciation to the soldiers for the price that they paid in fighting for their country, he passed a law making it legal for people with disabilities to beg in the street. As a result of this legislation, King Henry's soldiers went out into the street with their caps in their hands asking for money.

It didn't take long before the men with their "caps in hand" became known as the "hand and cap" army. From there, the term got shortened to simply "handicapped".

With that kind of history, it was easy to see how pejorative the word handicapped is. In the middle of the 20th century there was a movement to change the use of this term. "Handicapped" was a word that originated from the fact that individuals with disabilities were not seen as valuable contributors to society. The new buzzword became "disabled".

"Disabled" was intended to remove the stigma of people with disabilities being useless. The intention of using this new term was to show that this group of people, "The Disabled", had something that they could not do. It wasn't a judgment call, it was not a value statement, it was simply a description of how this group of people differentiated from other groups of people. It was pretty simple, there were limitations that they faced and they had certain limitations.

The problem arose when the label, "Disabled", became bigger than the person. Now, when people were being talked about, they were seen as a label, a descriptive, not as a person. By the end of the 20th century there was a movement to recognize people instead of labels. In this thought process, the concept of "Person First Language" arrived. Now, when people are referred to, the proper terminology is "a person with a disability". The idea of person first language is to recognize and affirm each individual's position as a person before applying any other label. The truth of the matter is that what defines us is our person-ness.

It was at this point in my lesson about language that I would explain my thoughts about the use of language. The fact is that I do not identify myself as being "handicapped". I don't identify myself as being "disabled". Neither do I define myself as being a "person with a disability".

I am Rob. I want people to know me for who I am. I don't want people to worry about what words they use when they talk about me. I want them to use my name when they talk to me. Political correctness can create a certain amount of fear and anxiety as people are trying to figure out what they can say that will not hurt or offend others. One way to ensure that you do not offend anyone with a disability is to find out what their name is and use it. Instead of talking about people, talk to them!

As I make this explanation, many members of my audience will nod their heads, they get it. I don't want to be labeled, I want to be viewed as me. It's important to be sure that we don't let the words we use get in the way of making a connection with the people around us.

After giving that part of my presentation across the country, I began to wonder if it was actually true. I hopped online to do some research. It turns out that as wonderful as the story about King Henry VII and the soldiers of old England sounds, it simply wasn't true. The use of the word "handicap" didn't originate until sometime in the 1600s. Even then, it had nothing to do with people having physical or mental limitations. It was related to a way to make things fair and equitable.

The first recorded use of "handicap" was in a form of trading. The trade would involve three people: two traders and a referee. Each trader would bring their trade item. The referee would determine the value difference between the two items and the trader with the lower valued item would have to chip in some money in order to make it an even deal. Essentially, the referee was "handicapping" the amount needed to equalize the value of the two items.

By the middle of the 1700s, it was being used in horse racing. They needed a way to bring the superior horses and the regular horses to an even playing field. To "handicap" the better horses, they added weights to their saddle. This meant that the stronger animals had to carry a heavier load than others.

It wasn't until the early 1900s that the term was used regarding children with physical limitations. I'm not sure why it was used. In it's original usage, it could be used because of a difference in how people are valued. In the horse racing sense, it could mean that people with disabilities were carrying a heavier burden than others. Even if it was some other reason, the fact is that it became a label that stuck and shaped the way we spoke and thought.

Here is how language impacts my life. The fact is that I do not identify myself as being "handicapped". I don't identify myself as being "disabled". Neither do I define myself as being a "person with a disability".

I am Rob. I want people to know me for who I am. I don't want people to worry about what words they use when they talk about me. I want them to use my name when they talk to me. Political correctness can help to keep us from unintentionally insulting people but it can also create fear and anxiety as people try to figure out what they can say that will not be hurtful or offensive. I have never been offended by someone calling me "Rob". There's no wrong way to take it.

"Rob Oliver" is the father of triplets. "Rob" is a best selling author and award winning speaker. Becky Oliver's husband is called "Rob". The kids at church call me "Mr. Rob". Why? because "Rob Oliver" encapsulates all of who I am. I'm not a label, I'm a person, I'm Rob Oliver!

(And I approve this chapter.)

Think about this:
1. Who are you?
2. What makes you unique?
3. What do you want people to think when they hear your name?

http://www.yourmotivationalspeaker.com/still-falling-videos/video9/

Chapter Ten

I Want to Hold Your Hand

It has always been interesting to me to listen to other people's thoughts about me and to watch the way they interact with me. Right after my injury, while I was still in the hospital, I would have friends that had known me since I was a kid come in and speak to me so very slowly. Sometimes, they would speak very loudly. "Hi Rob, do you remember me?" Of course I remembered them, I'd known them pretty much my whole life. Obviously, they thought that not only was I facing physical limitations but I was also facing mental limitations.

One of the things that happened on a fairly regular basis was my interaction with a guy from church. Every Sunday after our morning church service he would come over and say hello to me. He always wanted to know how I was doing and make sure that I was keeping well. I really appreciated his care for me. The problem was that whenever he wanted to talk to him, he felt that he had to hold my hand. Normally, this would not have been a problem. The big issue arose because he likes to hold my right hand which is the hand I use to drive the wheelchair and it was usually resting on the joystick of my power wheelchair.

Without fail, every Sunday he would come over and grab my hand which then meant he was holding both my hand and the joystick. As long as he held my hand still, we were fine but when he moved my hand, even slightly, the joystick moved as well. That movement caused the chair to roll forward a few inches, I felt a big bump and the run over his feet.

As I watched him, I could see the pained look cross his face. But he maintained a stiff upper lip, looking at me with sad eyes. I can't read minds, but his expression said, "That poor man just ran over my feet and he doesn't even know it." Of course, if you could read my mind, I was thinking, "That poor man just ran over his own feet and he doesn't realize it!" It was one of those situations where he thought that he was doing the right thing by not saying anything and I didn't have the heart to tell him that it wasn't my fault, it was his!

It took a little while before I finally got the solution to the problem. I don't like to turn my wheelchair off at all. It is my legs. Imagine that if every time wanted to go somewhere you had to turn your legs on and then wait for them to warm up before you could move. I don't have the patience for that, when I'm ready to go, I want to go right now. That being said, on Sunday morning, when I saw him coming towards me, I would immediately turn off my wheelchair. It saved both of us a lot of aggravation. Of course, it saved him a lot of pain as well.

The problems did arise again though. One Sunday morning my wheelchair was turned off but my hand was sitting on the joystick. When he grabbed my hand, he hit the power button for the wheelchair and in about 15 seconds it was turned on ready to go. His hand and mine were both on the joystick and away I went, right over his toes. I felt so bad for him as again he looked at me with this look of complete and total pity thinking just how sad it was that I didn't know what I had done to him.

I did explain to him that the problem stemmed from him touching the joystick but sadly, my explanation had no effect.

The way that he looked at me really bothered me. He thought I was stupid. He thought that I did not know how to operate my own wheelchair! In his mind, I was completely and totally socially unaware. It really hurt. Here I was, trying to do everything in my power to be gracious and keep him from being hurt and it really didn't matter. His opinion of me was not very high.

For many years I struggled with what people thought about me. Just because I have a disability doesn't mean that I'm stupid. Just because I have a disability doesn't mean that I am hearing impaired. As a matter of fact, having a disability doesn't really determine anything about me!

It wasn't until years later that I truly came to grips with what was going on. It was only then that I realized that his thoughts about me were in his mind and they had nothing to do with the reality of who I am. Just because someone thinks I'm stupid does not make me stupid. That perception is on them, it's not a part of me.

This type of scenario is played out over and over again in my life. There have been times when people made assumptions about me, misjudged me, demeaned me and discriminated against me. What I have come to learn is that prejudice and discrimination live with the individual who is judging, not with the individual who is being judged.

I am who I am. My intelligence, sense of humor, abilities, creativity, value and potential are not limited by the judgments of the people I encounter. Those traits are a part of me that cannot be taken away by anyone.

Prejudice, bias and stigma are things that we all deal with in our lives. The important understanding is that those items live in other people, they are not a part of you.

Think about this:

1. Have you ever accepted the limitations placed on you by others?

2. What are the valuable aspects of you that people miss because of their biases?

http://www.yourmotivationalspeaker.com/still-falling-videos/video10/

Chapter Eleven

The Vacation From…

Every year, in early June, our family goes for a week's vacation in Ocean City New Jersey. There are two things that I absolutely love about this trip. First, it's great to spend time together as a family. Second, Ocean City is close enough to Philadelphia that you can get a decent cheesesteak. While there are many wonderful things about living in Pittsburgh, it is impossible to get a good cheesesteak. Trust me, I have tried and they are just not the same!

Our trip in 2007 taught me a great deal. I was working two half-time jobs. They gave me my 40 hours per week and kept me busy. One offered vacation time, the other did not. As a result, I decided that I could only go for half a week. Becky and the kids went down on Sunday and I left to join them as soon as I finished my half-day of work on Wednesday.

Things started off badly when I arrived on Wednesday evening. My excitement at arriving and seeing everybody soon dissipated when Becky asked me, "Where is your suitcase?" I responded, "What suitcase?" It turns out that she had packed my suitcase and set it beside our bedroom door. Obviously, I didn't bring it.

In my defense, she didn't tell me that she had packed that suitcase for this trip. I had seen it, but she never specifically told me to bring that suitcase. Making assumptions is a huge problem and I had made the unfortunate assumption that she had taken my clothes with her on Sunday. She, on the other hand, had made the assumption that I would just know to bring that suitcase. Of course, I was imagining what would have happened if I had brought a suitcase that I was not supposed to bring.

The good news was that I had brought some of my supplies with me, separate from the suitcase. I had enough to get me through Wednesday night and into Thursday when I could go out and stock up on what I needed. I picked a few things up on Thursday morning and made my way back to our hotel. Everyone was down at the beach so I decided to visit a couple of places on the Boardwalk. I still had about an hour to kill before lunchtime so I drove my wheelchair the four blocks into town and checked out the bookstore, bakery and other shops.

When I arrived back at the hotel for lunch, my cell phone was not sitting on my lap where it had been all day. I checked everywhere to see if it had fallen beside my leg, onto my feet, onto the wheelchair, anywhere at all on my person. It wasn't there! My heart was in my throat and my stomach knotted up.

In hopes that someone had picked it up, I called it from Becky's cell phone. It rang, but then it went to voicemail. My only hope was to retrace my steps from my pre-lunch shopping trip. There went my plans to spend the afternoon with my family on the beach.

As I went on the Boardwalk, I looked at the boards, seeing if my phone was stuck in between any of them. I went back to every single place I had visited on the Boardwalk, checked the floors and asked the cashier if anyone had turned in a lost cell phone. No such luck. I headed into town and revisited each of my stops. The longer it took me to retrace my steps, the less and less hopeful I became. My last hope was to visit the information desk at the Boardwalk. They hadn't received any cell phones all day — to say I was disappointed would be a major understatement!

We decided to go to Becky's favorite restaurant for dinner, the Hula Grill. My plan was that I would just have to make do without my cell phone. I would spend the day with the kids on Friday and get my cheesesteak for dinner. At least that was my plan...

Friday morning I got up into my wheelchair to get dressed. I was moving across the room so that Becky could help me get my shoes and shirt on. What I didn't realize is that my bare feet were dragging on the floor. The toes of my left foot caught the carpet and tore the skin right where my toes connect to my foot. It was not real pretty!

I didn't want to go to the hospital. My plan was to spend the day with my family! I tried to convince Becky that I would be okay. We could dress it with a gauze pad and some Neosporin and that would heal up. Hesitantly, she went along with my idea. Ultimately though, we went to her parents' room for breakfast and when her mother saw the damage, she told me I had to go to the hospital.

I finally agreed to go but under one condition, I was going by myself. Why? Well, there are several reasons. First, we were on vacation. I didn't want anyone else to spend their vacation time at the hospital. Second, and more important to me, when I have someone with me, I get left out of the conversation. Instead of talking to me, the medical staff talks to my companion. The nurses ask them about my symptoms, my medications and my medical history. At that point, whoever is with me usually turns to me and repeats the question. I answer it and then the nurse asks THEM the next question. I'm the patient. I know the information better than anyone. They need to ask me the questions! Ultimately, to make sure that there are no glitches in the communication process, I have found that it is simply easier to go alone.

I arrived at the hospital by 9:00 a.m. I figured that in the worst case scenario I would be out of there by early afternoon. Then it was off to the beach. As things progressed, my figuring went right down the tube. I never saw the emergency room doctor until after

11:00. After about 30 minutes of examination and cleaning, he decided that it was beyond his expertise and that I needed to see a foot specialist. The foot specialist never showed up until after 1:00. It took him about 20 minutes to decide that he was not going to be able to stitch things up in the emergency room, I needed to go into the operating room.

Surgery was scheduled for 3:30. At 3:15 I was informed that an emergency case had come up and required use of the operating room. "THE operating room?" I asked. It turns out that the Shore Memorial Hospital only has one operating room. I had no choice but to wait.

And wait I did. I never got into the operating room until 9:30 that night. It only took about 45 minutes to get everything stitched up. But by the time I got dressed, back in my wheelchair and out to my van it was already 11:00 p.m. Thankfully, they had only use a local anesthetic so I was allowed to drive. (It was kind of weird to me. I can't feel my foot because of my spinal cord injury, yet they used a numbing agent. Go figure!) As I pulled out of the parking lot, I was feeling badly that my goal of spending the day with my family was completely shot. Since I hadn't eaten anything all day, I was hungry and wondered about the likelihood of any places being open where I could get a cheesesteak. I soon found out that the likelihood was none.

I consoled myself with a piece of Boardwalk pizza, which is probably second or third on my list of favorite things to eat other than cheesesteaks. Exhausted, I got in bed and tried to figure out how to salvage something out of this vacation. Our plan was to head home late morning on Saturday.

I was tired and a little cranky and couldn't think of any brilliant vacation savers. The only thing I came up with was a round of minigolf with the kids before we headed home. Unfortunately, there is only one accessible minigolf course on the Ocean

Boardwalk and it's old and plain. That being said, it's the only one I can go to and I decided to make the best of it. The kids and I set off down the Boardwalk, one sitting on my left leg, one sitting on my right leg and a third standing on the back of my wheelchair. We hustled through our game and made it back to the hotel just in time to load up in the van and head home.

I drove in silence, contemplating the events of the last few days. I didn't feel like talking, I was totally bummed out. This felt like the absolute worst vacation ever. I couldn't decide if there was even a point in being there! I was in worse shape now than before the trip. I now had no cell phone. I had a very nasty, stitched up wound on my foot. I hardly spent any time with my family. And, I didn't even get a cheesesteak!

When we arrived home, we got everything out of the van and sat down to eat dinner. Still feeling pretty low, I ate in silence. The kids were chatting away about all the things that they did while they were on vacation. I was glad that they had enjoyed themselves. My pity party came to a screeching halt when Becky's dad asked Josh, "What was your favorite thing about vacation?" Josh looked at him, cocked his head little bit and said, "Probably, playing golf with my dad."

There are probably a million different explanations for why he said that. At that moment, I didn't really care about why he said it. What I did care about was the fact that my presence on this vacation was the most important thing to my son. My perspective and attitude about the vacation changed 180 degrees. Suddenly everything was put into perspective. I discounted the minigolf outing, seeing all the reasons it wasn't "special". Josh enjoyed it because it was "dad time". That is priceless. Circumstances may be difficult, life may be hard, bad things may happen but the most important thing about life is the impact we have on the people around us.

Think about this

1. Who are the people in your life that you value?

2. What actions can you take to have a positive impact in their lives?

3. What effect does your attitude and behavior have on each person you meet?

http://www.yourmotivationalspeaker.com/still-falling-videos/video11/

Chapter Twelve

Brownies

What I'm going to say next is something that I never would have imagined saying, ever! I learned one of my most valuable life lessons in a sheltered workshop.

What is so weird about that? Let me tell you, I don't have a whole lot of positive things to say about sheltered workshops. To me, it's an antiquated and outdated idea that needs to be re-examined.

What is a sheltered workshop? It's a place where people with disabilities go to be "employed". The concept of people with disabilities being employed is fantastic! I am all in favor of everybody using their abilities to earn a living and contribute to the greater good. That being said, there's a good reason why I put employed in quotation marks.

In a sheltered workshop, the workers are paid by the piece instead of an hourly rate. This model allows for the employees to be paid significantly less than minimum wage. Let me give you an example. In one of the workshops that I visited, the employees were working together in a huge warehouse type room. It was well lit with high ceilings, cream walls and floor-to-ceiling windows along the wall that faced outside. There were several different stations throughout the warehouse. Among the activities that I saw was one individual who was running a T-shirt printing press, several individuals who were folding boxes, and a station where people were packing products into boxes. The individual that I had come to visit was sitting at a table near the back putting hooks on suction cups that would be used to hang sun catchers in the window. Each of the employees at the table had a box of hooks and a box of suction cups. They also had a large piece of cardboard in front of them with circles printed on it, 10 circles per line and 10 lines per page. Once they put the hook on the cup, it went into a circle. The grid made it simple to figure out how many pieces were completed, count the number of lines and multiply by 10.

Across the hallway from the workshop was a cafeteria for the workers. Our visit was just before lunch and the wonderful aroma coming out of the cafeteria caught my attention and made my mouth water. When asked about the lunch program, one of the staff members explained that they provide a hot meal for the workers that is healthy, delicious and affordable. Healthy was a concept I understood. Delicious was something that could be debated by each individual, according to their tastes. I was wondering about the definition of affordable. When I asked, I was told that the lunch costs $3.00. That sounded affordable to me. Actually, it sounded really affordable! Where else could you get a hot lunch for that cheap?

It wasn't until later in our visit that I realized that what is affordable to one person may not be to another. To me, $3.00 was a cheap lunch. To the workers in the workshop, that was a different story. As it turned out, several of the workers were in the red at the end of the day. The total amount that they earned over the course of the day was less than the $3.00 that they spent on lunch. This wasn't a matter of the lunch being too expensive, it was just that they were earning so little.

Let me say at this point that I do see some value in the workshops. First, it provides an opportunity for individuals with disabilities to demonstrate that they have marketable abilities. Second, they were started as a prevocational training ground for individuals with disabilities to build work experience (although, I'm not sure exactly what kind of job you are learning about by putting hooks on suction cups, but I digress.) Third, the individuals in sheltered workshops are getting out of their houses, interacting with others and doing something with their lives besides sitting in front of the television. It's a chance for people with disabilities to do something that they can take pride in and they can earn some money.

That being said, my visits to sheltered workshops were generally disappointing. I met people who had been in the workshop for years and years and it didn't seem like it was a plan to make this a prevocational, it had become their vocation. Many of the people that I met were working 20 to 30 hours a week and taking home less than $50 per week.

You can imagine my attitude when, after several years of sheltered workshop visitation, I was sent to visit a client who was working in a sheltered workshop. I was pretty sure it was going to be depressing and disappointing. I went in with the attitude that I was going to be totally bummed out by what I saw during my visit there. As it turned out, my client taught me one of the most amazing things that I've learned.

On the day that I met with her, she was putting lids onto travel coffee mugs. I don't know exactly how much she was paid per lid but I do know that she was at the workshop six hours a day, five days a week, and was bringing home less than $150 per month.

As we talked, I asked her questions to get to know her better. One of the things that she confessed to me is that she is a "junk food junkie". I asked her what she liked as far as junk food. She told me that she'll eat anything but really enjoys brownies. Then she clarified, "I really like the brownies that my neighbor makes." I had a mental image of her stealing the brownies off of the neighbor's windowsill while they were cooling and blurted, "How do you get your neighbors brownies?" I was hoping that she didn't say, "I steal them." Thankfully, she didn't. She told me that her neighbor gives her the brownies.

Intrigued, I asked, "Why does your neighbor give you the brownies?" She told me that her neighbor is older and has a dog. The dog is a big dog and it is so strong that when the neighbor walks the dog, it pulls her over. To help her neighbor, she walks the dog. She says, "I'm strong and the dog won't pull me over." In appreciation, her neighbor bakes her brownies and other snacks.

I was amazed. Here was somebody who had limitations. As far as other people were concerned she was not able to be competitively employed. According to her service provider the best that she could do was work in a sheltered workshop where she got paid by the piece. She had cognitive limitations and mental health issues. All these items were stacked against her, yet she was having a quality relationship with her neighbor.

The question was why? The lesson I learned that day was that everybody has limitations. Everybody has things that they can't do. Everybody has people that think that they are incapable. That being said, if you are willing to take your abilities and make the most of them, that's the foundation of independence, that's the heart of community.

Think about this:
1. Do you focus on your deficits or capabilities?
2. How can your abilities serve others?

http://www.yourmotivationalspeaker.com/still-falling-videos/video12/

Chapter Thirteen

Giving Directions

One of the things I have come to understand is that people have a certain amount of discomfort when dealing with people with disabilities. Is it okay to make eye contact? If I make eye contact for more than a few seconds will the person feel like I am staring at them? From birth, I have been a very outgoing person. My disability has not changed that at all. In fact, I feel as though it's my responsibility to reach out to everyone to alleviate some of the aforementioned discomfort. That means that as I travel on the street, I say, "Hello" to everyone. If I don't get a chance to say "Hi," I at least make eye contact and give a head nod.

When I started my job with the UCLID center, I was working in the Oakland section of Pittsburgh. Oakland is where the University of Pittsburgh is located as well as many of the University of Pittsburgh Medical Center Hospitals including, up until recently, Children's Hospital.

As you can imagine, between hospital staff, visitors, university students and local residents, parking is at a premium. The office building I was working in had a parking garage but it was difficult for me to use a parking pass to get in to the garage. The primary problem was that I use my hands to drive so I did not have a free hand to put the parking card in the reader. In order to have a free hand, I would have to put the van in park. My right hand is my stronger hand and when I tried to reach the card reader, I just couldn't get close enough. It would have worked if there was a parking attendant there to assist me but the garage was not manned. Another problem was making sure that there was a van accessible parking spot for my vehicle. The lift to get me in and out of the van is located on the passenger side and requires a large amount of clearance. Although I could technically park in any "Handicapped Parking Spot", I had to use one of the spots with a striped area beside so that there was room to deploy the lift. The parking garage was usually filled and more often than not, the accessible parking spaces were filled as well.

I talked to the director of parking for Children's Hospital and eventually we came up with a solution. Instead of parking at my office building, I would park at the main Children's Hospital building. They ran a valet service and would be able to make sure that I had a place to park. Now, they did not valet park my van. That would have been almost impossible because I drive from my wheelchair and there is no driver's seat. Additionally, the entire van is operated by a computer system. You don't have to be a rocket scientist to use it, but it does require some training. There were no accessible spots in the Children's Hospital garage but since the garage was staffed by the valets and the valets had keys to all of the vehicles, they could move vehicles in out to make sure that the parking spot next to my van was open. I was glad that I had a place to park and was assured that there would be space beside me to open the lift and get out of the van.

The good news was that I had a place to park. The bad news? It was three and a half blocks to get from where I parked to where I worked. That wasn't a big deal in the summer time. As a matter of fact, I enjoyed the sunshine as I rode down the sidewalk between the garage and my office. The big issue was when it was raining or, even worse, snowing!

During the first winter of this parking arrangement, I was complaining a little bit to one of the valets. While he was commiserating with my complaints, he told me that there was some connection between all of the hospitals and he thought I might be able to go through Children's Hospital, connect to several other hospitals and come out at my office building without having to go outside. Needless to say, my interest was piqued! After several inquiries, I found out that I could not get all the way to my office but I could get to the building right across the street. Unfortunately, nobody seemed to know exactly how to do it.

One snowy morning I headed into the office a little bit early, trying to make sure I allowed enough extra time for the weather and for any traffic delays it might cause. When I arrived, I had an extra 15 minutes before I needed to get to the office. That sounded like the perfect time to explore the "Inside Route".

I inquired at the Children's Hospital information desk to see if they could tell me how to get to the building right across the street from my office. The volunteer at the information desk did not know but told me that I could get to Presbyterian Hospital (the hospital that adjoined Children's) and ask their information desk. She told me that there was a hallway connecting the two hospitals on the fourth floor of Children's.

I took the elevator to the fourth floor set off down the hallway to Presbyterian. Eventually I found their information desk and asked how to go. The volunteer was not certain how to go the whole way but informed me that there was a skywalk that connected Presbyterian Hospital to Montefiore Hospital. To put an interesting wrinkle in the directions, even though I had come from the fourth floor of Children's, I was now on the first floor of Presbyterian. In order to get to the skywalk, I needed to go to the third floor. I figured that Montefiore was the next step in the direction I needed to go so I took the elevators up to the skywalk and set off to Montefiore.

Once I arrived in Montefiore, I looked around for a few minutes and could not find the information desk. Eventually I settled on asking the woman running the gift shop. She sent me to the elevators, where I went down one floor then followed a hallway to a bridge that connected to the building that I was looking for. Once I was there, I had to take the elevator down nine floors to the ground level where I could exit the building, cross the street and go into my office building.

I was very happy to know that there was indeed an "Inside Route" to get to the office. I finally had an escape from nasty weather and cold. All I had to do now was remember which floor I needed to be on in each hospital and which elevators took me to that floor. After two weeks, I was extremely comfortable with the route and could get to my office almost as quickly going through the hospitals as I could going down the sidewalk.

Empowered by my newfound geographical expertise, I soon found other connecting inside corridors to reach many of the other buildings in Oakland including the building where we conducted trainings. That was a huge find because the trainings were done at the top of "Cardiac Hill". The term "Cardiac Hill" is used for two reasons. First, it runs through the center of the hospital complex. Second, but perhaps more fittingly, it is so steep that climbing it may put you in cardiac arrest. The hill was steep enough that I was uncomfortable going up or down it in my wheelchair at anything close to full speed. I would only go at about half speed on my way up the hill and about 20% speed on my way down. Sandy, our administrative assistant, hated the hill because she had to carry all of our training materials up the hill to our sessions (as well as carry any unused materials back down the hill when we were done.)

By the time that I had been there for a year, Sandy decided that she wanted to learn the "Inside Route" to our training sessions. We loaded our training materials into a box and set out together. Since we were coming from the office, the directions were backwards. We crossed the street, entered the building, went up to the ninth floor, crossed the bridge and headed for the elevators to take us to the skywalk.

As we came down the hallway towards the elevators, we passed another bank of elevators. A woman was standing at the center of that bank with her hand extended but frozen about six inches away from the elevator button. As we went by, I made eye contact, nodded my head, smiled. She looked at me with a little bit of panic in her eyes. "Is everything okay?" I asked. She replied, "Is this the elevator that takes me down to Fifth Avenue?"

I told her that the elevator she was at did not go to Fifth Avenue. I pointed back down the hallway, told her to cross the bridge and take the elevator down to the ground floor where she would be on Fifth Avenue.

As I talked, she was nodding her head. I thought she was following along with what I was telling her. However, as soon as I was done, she turned to Sandy and said, "Is this the elevator that takes me down to Fifth Avenue?"

I chuckled quietly to myself as Sandy repeated exactly what I had just said. It was funny to me because Sandy had only been that way one time, just now, for the first time! I was the one that actually knew how to go. I was the one that was teaching Sandy how to go. Yet, somehow, my answer wasn't good enough.

Once Sandy was finished explaining the directions, the woman's face lit up, her look of panic disappeared, she grabbed Sandy's hand, said, "Thank you so much!" and headed down the hallway. I cannot find fault with a woman for saying thank you. It's one of those things that I have tried to teach my children. No matter how small the favor is that someone does for you, no matter how easy it was for them to do it, always say, "Thank you." That being said, I did wonder why she was thanking Sandy and not me. Why were Sandy's directions better than mine? No, as a matter of fact, they were exactly the same as mine.

I don't know what the problem was. It may have been that she was confused and hearing the directions for the second time cleared things up for her. Maybe it was because she was more comfortable hearing it from a woman. My suspicion is, right or wrong, that my directions were discounted because I was in a wheelchair. Sandy's directions were fine because she was standing.

A very weird mixture of emotions filled me. I wasn't angry necessarily, I was definitely irritated. More than that though, I was hurt. I am the expert. I have the knowledge. When the woman thanked Sandy, Sandy got credit for what I taught her. Sandy would not have known how to answer the woman's question if I had not showed her the route. The real kicker came as we walked away. Sandy asked me, "How did you know that she needed help? I didn't even notice her." The fact is that if I had not made the initial contact, the woman would have been stuck, standing at the elevator, not sure if she could get to Fifth Avenue. I was the one that reached out to her. I was the one that saw she was having a problem. I was the one that had compassion on her and asked her if she needed help. And for all my effort, I didn't even get a thank you. I didn't get anything. Sandy got all the credit and I got nothing.

As we made our way to the training, Sandy was shaking her head. She couldn't believe what had just happened either. The thing that amazed her was that the directions that she gave the woman were verbatim what I had said. Sandy told me that she really couldn't remember the route. All she could remember was listening to what I said and when the lady asked her for directions, she just repeated it back.

"You should go back and set her straight," Sandy said. I was steamed enough that I considered it. It was then that the situation came together for me. This was not about me. The reason I asked the lady if she needed help was not so that I could be a hero, it was because SHE looked lost. It was about meeting HER needs, not stroking my ego. What was important was not whether or not she knew that I was the expert, the geographical genius, the one that actually cared: it was about making sure that she got down to Fifth Avenue. Whether it was my directions or Sandy's, either way, we met her needs.

The lesson I learned is that helping others is not about you, it's about meeting their needs. It's not about who gets credit for providing the assistance. It's not about who has superior knowledge. It's not about who is the most helpful. It's not about any of those things! It's all about service. It's all about meeting other people's needs. I had to learn to let go of my pride and be satisfied with serving.

Think about this
1. Are you aware of people's needs?
2. What ways can you be of service to others?
3. Is your service about you or the people you help?

http://www.yourmotivationalspeaker.com/still-falling-videos/video13/

Chapter Fourteen

My Inadvertent Family

I am often amused by looks that I get, especially from children. What is even more amusing sometimes is the reaction of their parents! While the child is naturally curious, the parents react by saying, "Don't look." To me, talking to children is one of the most important things I can do. It forms the foundation for their understanding of dealing with people who are different. By interacting with children, I am able to show them that even though I am in a wheelchair, I have a personality and am basically just like everybody else.

Of course, talking to kids does have its drawbacks. For little kids, their eyes are drawn to the lights on the control panel for my chair and from there they reach out to grab the joystick. Once again, parents often react, "Don't touch that." In the case of really little kids, that works. With kids who are old enough to be taught, it is an educational opportunity to talk about "personal space".

There was one instance where being friendly and talking to kids put me in a weird situation. During my employment at Children's Hospital, I was traveling from one section of the hospital to another and had to take the elevator. As I waited, there was a woman and her two children standing beside me. One child was fairly small and she held him in her arms but the other child was about four years old and stood beside her, holding her hand. When I looked over, the four-year-old caught my eye and then immediately hid behind his mother's leg.

I wasn't sure if he was just shy around people or if it was my wheelchair but I thought this is a great opportunity to make a connection. He peeked out and I winked at him. He smiled and quickly hid again. It didn't take too long before he peeked out again and I asked him if he was having fun today. In the minute that we waited for the elevator, we had a brief conversation.

When the elevator did arrive, it was being run by an elevator operator. As we enter the elevator she looked at me and asked, "What floor are you and your family going to?" I told the operator which floor I was going to and then turned the mother and asked her what floor she was going to.

As the doors closed, I started to think about what the operator had said. Why did she think I was with my "family"? She did a really good thing in communicating with me instead of my "wife". I have definitely had the experience where people will not ask me questions, they will ask them to whoever I am with. That being said, that wasn't what happened here. She did talk to me but there was still something about what she said that didn't sit right.

I'm not sure where the thought came from but I started to wonder, "Did that elevator operator think that I could not be out by myself?" Did she assume that I must be out with my "family" because I could not be there by myself? Even the way she said "you and your family" was weird. Now, my mind was really going. She didn't think I could be independent. She didn't realize that I had driven my own vehicle to work. More than that, she didn't realize that I was not a patient, I actually work here! Her assumption about my "family" severely underestimated my abilities and independence. Did she assume that everyone in a wheelchair was a patient? Did she assume that everyone in a wheelchair must have had their "family" or someone else with them? Didn't she realize just who I am?

As quickly as those thoughts came into my mind, I started to think about how I could express this to the elevator operator in a way that would enlighten her for future experiences. I didn't want her to make these assumptions that everyone else that showed up using a wheelchair. My pride was going as well because I didn't want her to lump me in with every other wheelchair user that she had experienced. I had worked long and hard to become the man that I am. She did not realize who she was dealing with. "You and your family", she said. While I am very glad to have a family, I don't need to take them anywhere with me. I can get by completely on my own! By this point, I had worked up a good head of steam. I was going to use this as a great educational opportunity. The elevator operator would never make assumptions about anyone else in a wheelchair, ever again. I was going to set her straight!

Just before I opened my mouth, I realized that I was not wearing my hospital ID badge. While that was not a huge deal, it did make me realize that there was nothing about me to indicate that I was not a patient. As a matter of fact, the overwhelming majority of people that she dealt with were patients. Hospital staff were all in uniform or at least displayed some type of ID that they were hospital employees. Besides, she had not actually called me a patient. I was making a pretty big assumption myself!

On top of that, her assumption about me and my "family" was not that far fetched. If you saw two children, a man and a woman all standing together talking, it would make sense that they were family. Before I blasted her about assuming that this was my family, I had to realize that her assumption may not have had anything to do with me being in a wheelchair. It could have been as simple as the fact that we were all together and having a conversation.

My anger was subsiding quickly. I began to realize that I actually had no idea what was going on inside the elevator operator's mind. I could assume the worst, I could assume the best. Actually, I really shouldn't assume anything at all! My internal conversation had been all about me assuming what she was assuming about me. It occurred to me that if she was paying attention, she would see that we were getting off at different floors. The fact that I had asked the woman what floor she was getting off at indicated that we were not together.

Making assumptions is a natural part of being human. Most often, we do not take the time to gather all of the facts about a situation before we decide what we are looking at. People do not make assumptions purposefully. It takes a lot of effort to gather all the facts and sometimes we just don't have the time or take the time to do that.

Think about this
1. When do you make assumptions?
2. Why do you make assumptions?
3. What would change if you took time to consider the other person's perspective?
4. What impact do other people's assumptions have on you?

http://www.yourmotivationalspeaker.com/still-falling-videos/video14/

Chapter Fifteen

The Launch Ramp

One of my first jobs after graduating from Duquesne University was working with medical students to educate them about disabilities. Part of the training was provided by physicians but we felt that it was most important for the medical students to hear directly from people with disabilities before they left medical school and started to form any bad habits. We did a lunchtime lecture series where we brought in people with disabilities as well as medical professionals to talk about both sides of the situation. The individual would talk about the lived experience of having a disability and the medical professional would provide information about the more clinical aspects of the disability. Another training tool was a Journal Club where students and staff discussed scholarly articles about the interaction between disability and medicine.

We started off having those meetings in a classroom at the medical school and ordering pizza. After a few of those meetings, we decided to step up and move our Journal club meetings to local restaurants. Since I was doing some of the planning, I was able to ensure that each of the venues was accessible. Although, I will admit that my definition of accessible has changed somewhat. At that point, I was willing to settle -- mostly accessible was good enough.

One of the restaurants that were used was called Hemingway's. It was mostly accessible. It had a ramp going in the front door and the front of the restaurant was level with the ground. The problem was that the area that we met was at the back of the restaurant and was down one step. They had a piece of wood that they used as a ramp and it worked pretty well. It was a little bit steep, but it got me down to the proper level for the Journal club meeting.

One of the really cool things about my wheelchair is the seating component. It has what is called Tilt in Space. That means that the whole seat of the wheelchair can be adjusted. The back can be adjusted as well as the seat itself can be leaned back. The purpose of this is for pressure relief, but it also helps keep the chair balanced. When I went down the ramp to get to the meeting area, I just leaned the seat of the wheelchair back and it kept me from tipping over forward. (My wheelchair is a front-wheel-drive, which means that the larger wheels are in the front and the smaller wheels are in the back. As a result, if the chair is going to tip over, it will tip over forward.)

The one thing about my wheelchair that always bothered me was the device attached to the bottom of it that made it possible for me to drive my van right from my wheelchair. To make sure that my wheelchair did not move at all while I was driving my vehicle, there was a lockdown unit placed on the floor of my van. In order to lock down, my wheelchair had a bolt that was attached underneath. That bolt slid into the unit on the floor and locked in place to keep the wheelchair secure. The problem with that bolt was it really cut down on the wheelchair's ground clearance. It only cleared the ground by three quarters of an inch which made it very difficult to go over a bump of any size. It got caught on everything!

The fact that I was overly concerned about that bolt getting caught created an issue on this particular night. When the meeting was over, they put the ramp up and I got ready to leave. In evaluating the steepness of the ramp, I decided that if I went up frontwards the bolt was going to catch and I would get stuck. Therefore, the only thing that really seemed to make sense was to go up backwards. I was also worried that with the steepness of the ramp the wheelchair might not have enough momentum to get all the way up the ramp if I was going too slow. Logically, I felt the only way to make sure that I got up the ramp without getting stuck was to go fast.

I lined the wheelchair up with the ramp, turn the speed all the way up and backed up as quickly as I could. I hit the ramp going backwards at top speed and my entire world slowly turned upside down. I'm not really sure how long it took but it felt like a slow-motion movie. The back wheels hit the base of the ramp and popped up in the air. The front wheels acted like the fulcrum of a seesaw and the whole chair tilted forward. As I realized my mistake in calculation, the chair slowly continued to tilt forward until it passed the point of no return and I began to fall over onto my face.

It sounded like the entire restaurant gasped at the same time. Even though everything seemed to be going in slow motion for me, I still managed to hit the ground before anyone was able to reach me. It was surprising how gently the fall happened. Maybe it's the fact that I can't feel my legs. Whatever the case, I found myself laying face down on the floor with a large power wheelchair strapped to my back.

My boss and several of the medical students rushed over to me. They undid the strap that was holding me into the wheelchair and set the wheelchair back up right. Now I was no longer strapped to the wheelchair, however, I was still laying on the floor.

Several of the students reached down and grabbed my clothing to pick me up and put me back in the chair but I stopped them. I explained that we needed to have a plan and work together in order to make this happen. Eventually, we got four people to help out. They got me into a seated position on the floor then I put an arm around the two people on either side of me and the other two grabbed under my knees and on the count of three they lifted me up into the chair.

It took a few moments to get me put back in some semblance of order. Not surprisingly, my shirt was untucked and my pants were sliding down. Both of my shoes had fallen off as well. There was no mirror around so I had to trust the medical students that I looked okay.

As I drove home, I was vacillating between two emotions: embarrassment and outrage. I was supposed to be part of the training team for these medical students and here they were, having to pick me up off the floor and fix my clothing. Could I have been any less professional? I wondered, what did all the people in the restaurant think about me? I was worried about what would happen if I saw any of them in the future. Would they remember me as the guy that flipped my wheelchair over in the middle of the restaurant? And on that note, why did that restaurant have such a stupid system? And why were we using a restaurant that isn't completely accessible? Whoever thought that it would be okay to use a ramp that was so steep? And why didn't anyone grab me while I was flipping over?

As I was driving home, things began to come into focus a little bit more. Who made the decision to go up the ramp backwards? That would be me. Who decided to hit the ramp at full speed? Again, that would be me. Who gave the okay to use this restaurant in the first place? That would be yours truly! In thinking the whole thing through, I realized that the situation may not have been ideal but the primary reason that the wheelchair flipped over was operator error.

In my rush to get out of the restaurant, I had failed to think things through. In my effort to make sure that the bolt on the bottom of the chair did not catch, I failed to consider the overall design of the wheelchair. Ultimately, much of the reason I ended up on the floor was my own fault.

Sometimes, when we reevaluate the situation, we realize that it was not something that happened to us, it was something that we caused. In going through those difficult times, sometimes it's valuable to ask, "What was my role in this experience?" Understanding your own role is the key to ensuring that you don't repeat the same situation again in the future! It also keeps us from always blaming others.

Think about this:

1. Have you ever blamed someone or something for a situation that was your own fault?

2. How much difference would it make if you took a moment to "think things through"?

http://www.yourmotivationalspeaker.com/still-falling-videos/video15/

Chapter Sixteen

"Trust Me"

One of the privileges that I have through work is visiting Harrisburg on a regular basis. My preference is to make it a day trip whenever I can but sometimes I have no choice but to stay over. It's not that staying over is the worst thing in the world. Usually, I get to stay at the Harrisburg Hilton. It's a pretty nice hotel so there's no issue there to complain about. The problem is getting help while I am in Harrisburg.

When I am at home, I have everything that I need right at my fingertips. I have a regular schedule of attendant care lined up. All the equipment that I need is available, my routine is set. When I'm out of town, my Service Coordination provider helps me line up attendant care. The attendants are all very nice and professional. However, they are not My attendants. They don't know My care. They are not familiar with My situation. Every time that I get a new attendant, I have to walk them through every step of my care. Even when I have an attendant that I have used before, they haven't seen me in a few months and I have to refresh them on how to handle my care. It's not that I mind, it's just a hassle.

One of the big problems in finding attendants in Harrisburg has been transferring me from my wheelchair to bed. For the longest time all that we did was a manual transfer. That meant that the attendant had to actually physically lift me into bed. It's not as difficult as it sounds. At least that's what I think. Granted, I am 6' 2", weighed around 200 pounds and am by no means a lightweight. When I was in rehab I learned to instruct people in transferring me. It is amazing to me how good body mechanics and proper leverage makes the transfer easier than you would think.

In 2011 I came up with a solution to the transfer problem. Actually, I didn't come up with a solution, I just gave in to the reality that there are other ways to transfer me besides a "quad pivot". While I was visiting the Center for Assistive Technology, they used a Hoyer lift to transfer me. In my previous experience, a Hoyer lift sling was a piece of canvas that stayed underneath you for the whole time you were in your wheelchair. When you transferred into the chair, the sling just stayed with you until you got out. I didn't like that for multiple reasons. Number one, Becky has stressed to me that we cannot change the fact that I have a disability, we can make sure that I do not look "handicapped". Yes, I know that is stereotypical but I think you understand what I'm trying to say. Her point is simply that I need to look my best, all the time. Having the sling and its hooks hanging out around my wheelchair definitely creates a distraction from looking right at me. On top of that, having a sling underneath me for the whole day will affect how I sit. It will make me slouch in my wheelchair a little bit and may create some issues with skin integrity.

At the Center for Assistive Technology, they showed me a new kind of sling. It was designed to be removed after the transfer. As you can see from the picture, the large cushioned piece goes behind my back. The two straps that hang down go one under each leg and then they come up between my legs and connect to the lift. At first, I was a bit skeptical. There is nothing about that sling that goes underneath my backside. I am just held in by my legs and my back. There were definite questions in my mind about whether or not it was safe for me.

After using the sling a few times at the Center for Assistive Technology, I finally felt comfortable trying it out at home. My preference was still to do a manual transfer but the lift made everything easier on the attendants. If they weren't feeling up to a manual transfer, the lift was perfectly fine.

Once I had the sling and the lift, it became easier to find attendants on my trips to Harrisburg. It did not have to be someone with tremendous strength in order to transfer me, as long as they understood how to use a Hoyer lift, they were fine. All I had to do was bring the lift with me. Part of packing for the trip included putting the lift in the van. In order to secure it for transit, we would literally seat belt it into the back bench.

It turned out that the lift was not a problem for any of my attendants in Harrisburg, the sling was. It seems like none of the attendants were familiar with how to put me into the sling. I felt like it was pretty straightforward. I tried to explain how the large part went behind my back. It was important to put that part down as low as possible. The strap on the right side when under my right leg and came up through the middle. The strap on the left side went under my left leg and came up through the middle. There were four hooks on the lift. Each leg strap got a hook and the loops on either side of the back piece each got a hook. It was then a matter of pressing the button and watching the lift pick me up.

My first few trips with the lift went pretty well. Let me clarify, by "pretty well" I mean that I did not fall out of the lift. There were times I felt like I was slipping a little bit but I always made it safely to my destination, whether that was the chair or the bed.

Let me just say that there is one trip in the spring of 2014 that I will not forget for a very long time. I had worked with several attendants previously and they got to know me and my routine a little bit. On this particular trip, I got a new attendant. She was exceptionally nice. She was in her 20s and had moved to the United States from Africa. We had a great conversation while she explained that she really enjoyed the work that she did. She found great satisfaction in helping people who needed her assistance.

Once everything was unpacked, she helped me get ready for bed. I brushed my teeth, washed my face and got out the lift. As the attendant picked up the sling, she turned it over in her hands a few times looking very perplexed. She had never seen one like this. I explained how it worked and we started to get it set up. The large piece went by my back, the two straps went under my legs, they crossed and everything got connected to the lift.

As the lift started to go up, something didn't feel right. Instead of the leg straps being under my thighs, close to my hips, they slid down and were underneath my knees. My fear about having nothing under my backside was truly realized at this point. Usually, there was enough support with the leg straps and back rest that I couldn't move it at all. With the leg straps being at my knees, there was a giant hole and I started to slide down.

The only thing I could think to do was wrap both of my arms around the leg straps in front of me and hold on for dear life as she moved to the left towards the bed. When I did this, I lost pressure against the back piece and now the only thing that was keeping me in the left was the straps underneath my knees and my arms wrapped around the leg straps. I was worried, my attendant was worried, it was not looking good.

Having limited arm strength meant that I was not going to be able to hold on for long. It only took a minute or so before my arms started to shake. I told the attendant that I was not sure how much longer I was going to be able to hold on. My arms slipped a little bit and my heart leapt into my throat. I tried to readjust my grip but every time I moved, I slid little bit further down. It was at that point that something totally unexpected happened. The attendant came over beside me and grabbed under my knees and under my arms. She said, "I have you." I told her, "I am really heavy and I can't help you." She said, "Trust me."

I didn't have a lot of choice. I could trust myself and try and hold on but it was just a matter of time before my arms gave out and I fell through. We didn't have enough time to get someone else to help us. The choice was pretty clear, I had to trust her.

The next thing I knew, she lifted and I landed on the bed. It was a tangled mess of me, clothing, sling, bed sheets and her but I was on the bed. To say I was relieved was an understatement!

I came to realize that in my mind, I had multiple reasons why there was no way she would be able to lift me up into bed. I had logic and reason on my side. Rational thought dictated that there was no way that she would be able to pick me up. There were oh so many reasons why I should not have trusted her to lift me. Yet, in spite of all of those instincts and reasons, she had put me in bed. She saved me from falling on the floor. She asked me to trust her and then followed through on her promise. Sometimes, when you are faced with the limits of your own strength it's time to let go and trust someone else!

Think about this:
1. Are there times when you are unwilling to let go?
2. Are you willing to completely trust someone else?
3. What has amazed you when you trust others?

http://www.yourmotivationalspeaker.com/still-falling-videos/video16/

Chapter Seventeen

My Name Is... Bob??

Getting my speaking career started was hard. It's not easy to get booked as a speaker for conferences when you are not well known. Building a speaking business from nothing takes a lot of time and effort. For me, things started off with speaking for free to local service clubs like the Rotary, Lions Club and Chambers of Commerce. As things built up, I moved on to bigger audiences and (thankfully) presentations that actually paid.

I don't think there is any way to accurately describe the excitement that I had about finally being paid to speak. Speaking to larger audiences was exhilarating. People were finally starting to take me seriously as a speaker.

One of my first paid gigs was a learning experience. The first few nights after I was booked, my mind was running away with thoughts about how my presentation was going to be received. I would stare into the darkness and think about my outline. Throughout the night I was coming up with all types of great stories and powerful quotes that would have a lasting impact on the audience.

The next phase of my sleeplessness came as I mulled over the logistics of exactly what I needed to do at the conference. To PowerPoint or not to PowerPoint? That was the question!

The final week before the presentation, my sleep was disrupted by a whole new set of issues. As I lay awake, my mind ran through scenarios about what could go wrong. What if I got sick? What if they didn't have a projector? What if we got a blizzard? What if I couldn't get to sleep at all until after the conference? What if I was unable to stop asking "What If" questions? The questions spiraled into a very unproductive place. I simply could not wait to get to the conference, wow them with my speech and be done worrying about "What If".

Upon my arrival at the conference, my worries became reality. They were delighted to meet me but then they pulled out my name tag. It was preprinted with a sticker on it denoting that I was a speaker. It was professional and it looked sharp, but it had a mistake on it. Instead of saying "Rob Oliver", it said "Bob Oliver".

What was I to do? The meeting planner very kindly assisted me by attaching the name tag to my sweater. This was my first chance to meet her face to face. Should I tell her that she made a mistake? No, that would be terrible. I was hoping to make a good impression on her so she would hire me for future presentations, give me a referral or provide a testimonial letter. If I insulted her first thing after meeting her in person, the chances of any of that happening dropped.

Now my mind was racing in another downward spiral. Once I left the meeting planner, maybe I could get rid of this name tag. Wait, that wasn't going to work. I needed the name tag to show that I was a speaker. Maybe I could take out the prewritten name tag, turned it over and write my name on it correctly. No, that's a bad idea too. My handwriting is terrible. Maybe I could get someone else to do it?? But, I don't know anybody at this conference (except the meeting planner and I certainly wasn't going to ask her.) I thought about keeping my hand over the name tag and introducing myself correctly but the name tag was too high up to easily keep it covered. I resigned myself to the fact that I was just going to have to deal with it.

My self-consciousness was through the roof. As I made my way through the conference attendees, I tried to seem as confident as possible, smiling and making eye contact, hoping people would simply nod back and that would be the end of it. That worked for a while but then someone spied the speaker tag. The gentleman stuck out his hand and introduced himself. He looked at my name tag and my heart sank as he said, "It's very nice to meet you Bob." Before I could react he called out to one of his coworkers, "Hey, come here, I want you to meet our speaker, Bob Oliver."

When I looked at the program, things got worse. There, in black and white print, the keynote speaker was listed as "Bob Oliver". Begrudgingly, I wondered if I would have to settle for being called "Bob" for the rest of the conference. This was definitely not going to help build my brand. Googling "Bob Oliver" was definitely not going to find my website or videos. Searching Amazon for a book by "Bob Oliver" was definitely not going to come up with my book.

I decided to take matters into my own hands. In a coat room beside the main auditorium I found a little privacy. Hiding there gave me a few minutes alone to remove my name tag which wasn't easy. It took several minutes to unhook the pin that held the tag to my sweater. Getting the pin out of my clothing was another struggle, but after a few moments — Mission Accomplished!

My next move was to find out who was going to do my introduction. It didn't take long to make sure that my name was correct throughout the introduction. The cool thing was that when the guy who was doing my introduction found out what had happened he took it upon himself to explain that there was a misprint in the program. That allowed me to make a joke about the whole thing. (It was lame, but it was a joke after all. "Bob backwards is Bob. Rob backwards is 'Bor' and I hope that my presentation is anything but that.")

At home that night, I lay in bed thinking. My hope had been that I would be able to sleep much better now that the event was over: no worrying about what I was going to say, no worrying about my PowerPoint, and no worrying about what else could go wrong. But I still couldn't sleep. My mind kept going over the whole "Bob" thing. For starters, I'm not going to sign a contract with my full name "Robert" again. If I write "Rob" on the contract, it should eliminate the confusion in the future.

The next series of realizations blew my mind. The name tag was a label. I realized that the label that was put on me was constructed by someone else. They had good intentions in creating it but they didn't realize what the content of the label meant to the individual who was going to be wearing it. On top of that, I thought about why I was afraid to take the label off. There were many reasons why I was afraid: social pressure, fear of speaking up, not wanting to stick out, and the position of the individual who had created the label. I realized that my complacency in accepting the label meant that others believed that the label was true. Finally, I realized that in this instance and in every other instance where a label is put on me, the only person responsible for removal of that label is me.

Think about this
1. What labels have been (incorrectly) stuck on you?
2. What did you do about them?
3. How will you handle inaccurate labels in the future?

http://www.yourmotivationalspeaker.com/still-falling-videos/video17/

Chapter Eighteen

The Trip From...

The voice on the other end of the phone asked, "Where are you?" The tone was angry. The person asking the question was my supervisor. She was definitely not a person that I wanted to make angry and, furthermore, someone that I had never seen get angry! However, the way her question came across, it was apparent she was angry. Normally, I would have responded with something that would calm her down but, you see, I was angry too. My response was matter of fact and abrupt, "I am on my way and will be there shortly."

In order to understand the situation, you need to understand what led up to it. It really started weeks before. Our organization was concerned about the residents of a nursing facility in the Philadelphia area. After several meetings, it was determined that three people needed to visit the facility: me, my supervisor and one other staff person from the Harrisburg office.

I was irritated by this. We have an office in Philadelphia. We have an office in Harrisburg. Did it really make sense for me to travel all the way from Pittsburgh to Philadelphia for a two hour visit? Really, it meant that I was going to have to travel over 700 miles. It meant that I was going to be away from my family for two days. It meant that I had to stay in a hotel overnight (which is a bigger deal than it sounds like.) It meant that I would have to arrange for attendant care services during my hotel stay.

To me, it made more sense to use the staff in the offices that were closer. However, that was not the plan. This wasn't about what made sense to me. It was a plan from management. The decision was for me to go. My responsibility was to make the necessary plans for my part of the visit.

We were scheduled to go to the nursing facility on a Tuesday. We were going to meet at the facility at 9:30 a.m. which meant I had to travel out the day before. Usually, when I go out to visit in Philadelphia, I stay with my parents who still live in the area. It's always good to spend time with them. Unfortunately, for this trip they were going to be out of town. As a result, I made hotel reservations and contacted an attendant care agency in the Philadelphia area to make arrangements to have someone help me get into bed on Monday night and out of bed on Tuesday morning.

Making the hotel reservations was not a big deal. Most of the chains have rooms that are specifically designed to accommodate wheelchair users. Arranging for attendant care was a little more complicated. I contacted several agencies in the Philadelphia area to see if they had any attendants in the area of my hotel. The first five agencies that I contacted had no one. Finally, the sixth agency had someone that could help me! In order for them to assist me, they had to open a case for me. That sounded reasonable to me until I found out what was entailed. Before the attendant could come out to my hotel, I had to meet with a nurse from their agency who would do an assessment of my needs. That went from a minor imposition to a major irritation when I found out that the assessment was going to take an hour!

Are you kidding me? An hour assessment? I needed two hours worth of help on Monday night and two hours worth of help on Tuesday morning. That's a total of four hours! And yet we need to do an hour-long assessment? I wanted to find someone else to work with but two things became apparent after contacting four more agencies. First, none of the other agencies had staff close to my hotel. Second, any of the agencies that did have staff close to the hotel were unwilling to take me on as a client because I only needed four hours. That meant that my choice was to endure the hour-long assessment or stand my ground and risk the possibility of not getting coverage. Frustrated, with a sense of resignation, I arranged to meet the nurse at my hotel at 7:00 p.m., an hour before the attendant arrived.

Once the schedule was in place, I reverse engineered my travel plans. At a decent rate of speed, it would take about five hours to get there so I needed to leave my house by 2:00 in the afternoon. One of my good friends lived not too far from the hotel so I thought about getting dinner with him and his family. If we had dinner at 5:00, that meant I needed to leave around noon.

I texted my friend and arranged to meet him and his family for dinner. Since we were going to be near Philadelphia, I requested that we have cheesesteaks. I didn't care where we got them from. My personal experience told me that most of the local "Mom and Pop" pizza places made pretty good cheesesteaks. Furthermore, my personal experience told me that you can't get a true Philly cheesesteak anywhere other than the Philadelphia area.

That plan fell to pieces when my supervisor requested that we have a phone call at 1:30 on Monday afternoon to go over plans for the nursing facility visit. She had some documents for us all to review which meant that I was going to have to be in front of my computer for the call. So much for leaving at noon!

Shortly after 1:00 on Monday afternoon, I got an email stating that we were going to have to push the phone call back until 2:00. I figured that the call would take at least 30 minutes which meant I was definitely not going to be on the road by 2:00 either!

The call took 40 minutes. As soon as it was over, I hit the road. I had printed out directions to the hotel which estimated my travel time at 4 hours and 50 minutes so I knew I had to put the pedal to the metal. For the next four hours, I drove like I was trying out for

NASCAR. It was effective too! I shaved 50 minutes off my trip, pulling into the parking lot at 6:40.

I was relieved to know that I had 20 minutes before the nurse was going to show up. When I realized what I had to accomplish in that 20 minutes, it became very apparent that I only had 20 minutes to get checked in, bring in my suitcase, check out the room for accessibility and (most importantly) order some dinner. Check in went quickly. They offered free Wi-Fi and the desk clerk provided me with the connection code. I also got some menus for local places that had good cheesesteaks. The bellboy helped me bring in my suitcase and the Hoyer lift. Before he left the room, we measured up the bed to make sure that the legs of the lift would fit underneath it. They would not.

The bellboy contacted maintenance to see what could be done to raise the bed off the floor. It took a little while to figure out what the hotel had on hand that could be used. Eventually, we decided that we could put plastic soda cases under each corner of the bed which would allow enough clearance for the lift. The maintenance man headed off to round up four soda cases. In the meantime, I input the Wi-Fi codes into my iPad and my iPhone, texted Becky to let her know that I was safe and ordered a cheesesteak to be delivered by one of the local pizza places. When the maintenance man returned, he put the soda cases under the corners and we tested to see if the lift would fit. It did! To let him know how much I appreciated his help, I found a copy of "Still Walking" in my luggage and signed it for him.

Just as he was finishing, there was a knock on the door and the nurse arrived. Even though it didn't make sense to me that her assessment was going to take an hour, it sure did! She wanted to know all kinds of information about when my injury occurred, the level of my injury, my medications, my family arrangements, my living arrangements, my employment, the assessment went on and on and on! Around 7:50, we were finally wrapping up the assessment when I got a call from the front desk that my food had arrived.

The nurse finished her questions and I walked her out to the lobby. The deliveryman was waiting there with my food so I paid him and headed back to my room. It smelled delightful! Inside the room, I opened up the bag and spread out "the goods": my coveted cheesesteak and an order of fries. I unwrapped the sandwich but before I had a chance to take a bite, there was another knock on the door. It was my attendant, she was a few minutes early.

While this really wasn't a big deal, it did make things a little bit awkward. She couldn't go home until she was done helping me. She couldn't start helping me until I was done eating. There was really nothing for her to do while I was eating except sit and watch me. In order to get through this awkwardness as quickly as possible, I shoveled my cheesesteak down. This is not about enjoying the sandwich, it was about getting it into my body so we could move on to the next step.

While I was eating, I asked my attendant questions. I was hoping that the time would move more quickly for her if she was talking. She informed me that she was from the islands. I'm not sure how the topic came up but she told me that she was a Christian and enjoyed going to church. She told me about her kids and her grandkids and by that time I was done eating. Okay when I say that I was done eating, I had finished the cheesesteak and eaten a couple fries and decided to let the rest of them go to save time.

We started the process of getting me ready for bed: brushing my teeth, washing my face, getting out my clothes for the next day, and getting the lift all set up. Once that was done, we took my shirt off and I was ready to get in bed. We had the sling underneath me and hit the button to lift me up. As I went up, the sling slid down to my knees and my backside began to slide out of the lift. I grabbed a hold of the straps and held on for dear life. The attendant did not know what to do. She was praying out loud, "Help me Jesus!" I told her that we needed to get the lift up as high as possible so that my backside would be higher than the bed that we could just slide me over. She followed my instructions but when the lift got to its highest point, I had slid down far enough that I still could not clear the edge of the bed.

The muscles in my arms were getting tired. As we tried to figure out what to do, my arms started to shake and slip. I readjusted my grip but it was to no avail, my strength gave out and I let go. My knees stayed in the sling but my torso slid through the opening. As soon as my shoulders slid through the opening, my head smacked on the legs of the lift.

So there I hung. My head was thumping. My knees were still in the sling which meant I was hanging upside down. Somehow, in the course of everything my pants got pulled down to my knees. My attendant went from being in prayer to letting loose a string of profanities. She put her hands on her head and stood there, staring at me, muttering, "What am I going to do? What am I going to do?"

What happened next was very surreal. I asked her if she was okay. She didn't answer my question but just kept muttering. I asked if she was hurt. She shook her head, no. I told her that I was glad that she was okay and that we would get through this. She nodded her head and then looked at me and asked, "What am I going to do?" I told her to call the front desk and tell them that we needed help. She picked up the receiver on the phone, stared at the numbers and waived her index finger in a circle over them. "What do I do?" She asked. When I told her to call the front desk, she informed me that she did not have her glasses on and could not read the numbers. I told her to bring the phone over to me and I would tell her which button to push. Of course, she had to hold the phone upside down because I was still hanging from the lift.

She was so flustered by the whole experience that once she did get connected with the front desk, she didn't know what to tell them. I had to tell her, one sentence at a time, to let them know that I had fallen and we needed help.

As we waited for help to show up, I asked her to lower the lift. It had only come down about a foot before my legs finally slipped out of the sling and I fell to the ground. It was at that point the maintenance man came to the door. It was not until after the attendant let him into the room that I realized just how uncomfortable I was with this whole situation. I was laying almost naked on the floor of a hotel room with two total strangers.

As he worked together with the attendant, we all talked and decided that it would be best for the two of them to do a dead left from the floor to the bed. He grabbed under my shoulders and she grabbed under my knees. The maintenance man did most of the lifting and I ended up safely in bed.

At that point, the maintenance man left and the attendant finished getting me ready for bed. She helped plug in my iPhone so it would charge overnight. There was no plug available on my side of the bed so she ended up plugging it in to an outlet on the desk across the room from me. I had brought my iPad with me which was fully charged so I could text and communicate through FaceTime. Before the attendant left, I made sure that I had correctly input the Wi-Fi code from the front desk.

Once the attendant left, I took a few minutes to think over what a crazy day it had been. I called Becky to let her know that I was safe, that I loved her and to tell her about my experiences. When I finished my phone call with her, my iPad somehow got disconnected from the Wi-Fi. Unfortunately, the card with the code on it was on the other side of the room with my phone. For

20 minutes, I entered and re-entered the code as best I could remember it but could not get it right (when I double checked in the morning, I found out that I was off by 1 digit.) That meant that I was now alone in a hotel room five hours away from home with no way to communicate with the outside world.

The next morning, my alarm went off at 6:55 so I would be awake when my attendant arrived at 7:00. She didn't. As a matter fact, she didn't show up at 7:15 or even 7:30. Now my lack of communication ability became a major concern. My mind raced, "What if she forgot about me?" I was very unsure of what I was going to do. I began listening as voices passed by my door. I thought about calling out to them for help. My mind was a sea of anxious thoughts and prayer.

At 8:00 I heard somebody opening my door. My initial concern was that it was housekeeping coming into clean up my room. I was glad to have someone coming in but that was going to uncomfortable. It turned out to be my attendant. She was under the impression that she was coming from 8:00 until 10:00 on Monday night and from 8:00 until 10:00 on Tuesday morning. Her hours for Monday were okay, my request for Tuesday had been from 7:00 until 9:00.

The good news, bad news scenario continued. This was the same attendant who had been there last night and dropped me. That made me a little uncomfortable. On the other hand, the fact that she had dropped me would encourage her to be more cautious in getting me up out of bed. I didn't have much choice in the matter, she was there and was pretty much my only option for getting ready for the day.

We hurried as much as possible. Incredibly, she got me dressed and out the door to my van in just over an hour. Now, I had to move as quickly as possible to get from my hotel to the nursing facility. Traffic was horrific and it felt like I was getting every red light possible. In the middle of all this, I was trying to read my directions, read street signs and make the correct turns.

I was sitting at a red light, trying to read the name on the cross street because I was pretty sure I missed a turn and that's when my phone rang. The angry voice on the other end of the phone asked, "Where are you?" I had to take a deep breath. I was frustrated, I was angry, I was tired, I was stressed. My initial thought was self-justification but I decided to hold back and simply answer the question. Through clenched teeth I said, "I am on my way and will be there shortly."

The rest of the ride went slowly. My frustration was now mixed with a sense of impending doom. I was not sure why she was mad, I was hoping it wasn't anything I had done. When I arrived at the facility, I was surprised that the only member of our organization that was there waiting for me was our deputy director. When I asked her if we were going to wait for the other person to join us, she shook her head no. "Is she okay?" I asked. It was at this point that I found out why she was angry when she called me. Apparently, she arrived before 9:30. She called my coworker to get an ETA and my coworker forgot about the visit! Since I wasn't there, she worried that I had forgotten as well, hence the frustration in her voice when she called about where I was. It wasn't about me at all. It was about an unfortunate circumstance. It was about frustration with another person altogether. However, since I was the next one up on the phone, it came through to me loud and clear.

I apologized for being late and shared the events of the morning to explain why I was not there exactly at 9:30. Her face softened as she heard the details. She commented that I had been having a rough day already and it was only getting started.

Looking back, I realize that both of us were extremely frustrated with the circumstances surrounding us and let that set the tone for our conversation with each other. Her frustration with my coworker carried over into her next phone conversation which just happened to be with me. I allowed my experiences from the previous day and weeks to affect my thought patterns.

The solution was finding out what was going on with the other person. Once I understood my supervisor's experience, her frustration was understandable to me. After hearing the story of my morning, she was actually empathetic. We didn't hold hands or sing Kumbaya, but we each understand the other's perspective.

I learned to be aware of my own stress level. It has an impact on my interactions with other people, my decision-making, my reactions. Decisions made under stress are not well thought out, they are reactionary. By being aware of my stress level, I can remind myself to think before reacting.

On top of that, I learned that other people are going through difficult circumstances. By listening to them, not only can we empathize with them, we can understand some of the rationale for their behaviors. Hopefully, it made me a little more gracious in the way that I look at other people and understand their actions.

Think about this:
1. How does stress impact your decision-making?
2. How do you perceive others when they are under stress?

http://www.yourmotivationalspeaker.com/still-falling-videos/video18/

Chapter Nineteen

Discrimination? Maybe not!

    Obstacles are all around us. We all face limitations each and every day. One of the things I learned to look at is the source of those obstacles. Sometimes, people say and do things because they are not aware of the entire situation. Other times, people operate based on stereotypes and misinformation. Sometimes, the obstacles we face come from totally unexpected sources.

    A favorite training workshop of mine is about advocacy. It's called "This Stinks and It Needs to Be Changed!" It comes from my experiences personally as an advocate as well as working with self advocacy groups. It's all about how to get your message across.

    There is one small self advocacy group that stands out in my mind. I started working with them from the day I got hired at Disability Rights Pennsylvania. The group consisted of four primary members and several people who would come and go over the course of time depending on what issues they were facing. It was here that I learned about the various sources of adversity.

    The group was looking at several issues of concern around the city they lived in. One of their primary issues was physical access to local businesses and government offices. They were also looking at accessibility to polling places as well as ensuring that the local Department of Public Works was installing curb cut ramps in compliance with the ADA (Americans with Disabilities Act.)

    Jeff, one of the group leaders, was an individual who had, among other disabilities, a traumatic brain injury. He often shared stories about how difficult his life was, especially because, as an individual with a disability he was facing constant discrimination. This wasn't just people looking at him funny, this wasn't just mild discrimination, no way, this was major, hate filled, vitriolic discrimination.

One meeting, Jeff really opened up and shared four stories, back, to back, to back, to back, chronicling the horrific treatment that he received because of his disability. There were two of those stories that still stick out in my mind.

The first story took place during roadwork season. For those of you not from Pennsylvania, we have two seasons. There is Winter and then there is Road Repair. Sometimes, Winter gets shortchanged as we do road repair then as well.

The Americans with Disabilities Act has a provision regarding accessible sidewalks. Any currently existing sidewalks are okay to remain inaccessible but as the roads around are repaired, the sidewalks must be brought up to standard. The easiest way to explain this is that when they are re-paving the road, they must put curb cut ramps at every intersection that they come to. It's a great concept. It means that the cost of making the sidewalks accessible is factored into the cost of paving the road. Instead of there being two lines in the budget for the separate issues, it's all rolled into one. Whoever does the repaving has to ensure that the curb cuts are being placed.

Jeff and the rest of the advocates felt that their town was not actually living up to this standard. They were concerned that repaving projects were being conducted but the curb ramps were not being installed. Somehow, they got a list of all of the paving projects going on in the town and decided to go check on the sites to see what was going on.

It was a project that Jeff was totally excited about. Armed with a list of the paving projects and a digital camera, he set off around town to gather photographic evidence of where the ramps were not being properly installed. It was a well conceived project and it definitely carried the right idea of documenting where the town was violating the law. It's hard to argue with photographic evidence!

    This is where the story took a turn. For some reason, someone alerted the police about Jeff and his project. He had only visited four or five intersections and taken a handful of pictures before one of the local police officers showed up to inquire about what Jeff was doing. One of the group members interrupted the story and asked Jeff what was the officer's name. When he mentioned the name, their reaction was, "Oh, good, he usually understands where we are coming from." Jeff responded that the officer must have been having a bad day. He went on to explain that during the course of his explanation about what he was doing and why he was doing it there arose some contention between himself and the officer. Okay, maybe contention is not a strong enough word. Strife is not a strong enough word either. It quickly escalated from misunderstanding to argument to conflict. A big enough conflict that by the end of it, the officer had drawn his gun and was pointing it at Jeff telling him to stop doing what he was doing, get back in his car and go home!

    Jeff was incensed the officer's lack of understanding, lack of compassion and overt discrimination. He decided to, reluctantly, go along with what the officer said but not before he had written down the officer's badge number, car number, the date, time and address of the incident. He also took pictures of the officer and his vehicle. After that, he did get in his car and went home.

    Jeff's question after the story was, "What happened to that officer understanding us? What happened to him being on our side? I can't believe he treated me that way." Apparently, the question was merely rhetorical. He did not wait for any response but immediately launched in to his next story.

This story was about polling place accessibility. One of the most powerful ways for individuals with disabilities to give weight to their political views and requests of government officials is to be registered to vote and be an voter. In order to be an active voter, you have to be able to get into your polling place and access the voting machines.

The Pennsylvania Department of State has a checklist identifying everything that needs to be accessible at each polling place. The group had a copy of this and Jeff took it as a personal mission to check out the polling places in his area. One of those polling places was a fire station. Armed with the accessibility requirements check list and his digital camera to document all noncompliant items, Jeff cased the establishment.

His interactions with the staff of the firehouse did not go well at all. Apparently, the staff was frustrated enough with him that they decided they would not deal with him at all. The only person that would deal with him was the fire chief. Once again, I was not privy to exactly what the conversation was between Jeff and the Fire Chief. I will say that it did not go well! Actually, things went straight downhill like a greased alpine slide. The Fire Chief's anger and his statements became increasingly stronger. He went from "don't bother my staff" to "your survey is now over" to "get off the property".

I could not believe my ears when Jeff told us how bad things got. Apparently, at the end of the conversation, the Fire Chief told Jeff, "I hope that one day when you go into cardiac arrest the call comes in our emergency medical transport unit. It will be my pleasure to get onto the ambulance, ride out to your house and watch you die!"

After listening to all the stories, it was apparent that they all had a similar outcome. People were discriminating against him in the most vehement of language and with the most vicious of statements. To Jeff, it was obvious that discrimination is rampant in his town and community. For me, it was something different.

I told Jeff that I felt very badly that people had treated him that way. I agreed that it must be terribly hurtful to hear such mean things being said about him and to him. It was my next statement that put a major damper on my relationship with Jeff moving forward.

I told him that all of the stories that he told today had one thing in common, him. The people that were discriminating changed, the circumstances in which they were discriminating changed, the reason why they were discriminating changed overall, the one constant was him. I challenged him with the question, "Is it possible that people are angry at you and your personality and that it has zero to do with your disability?" I do realize that a brain injury can have an effect on communication, emotion, and social understanding. It's possible that his brain injury made his interaction with these individuals difficult. That being said, they were discriminating against him not because he had a disability, they were angry at him because of the way that he treated them and the manner that he conducted himself.

Jeff was highly insulted at my suggestion. There was no way that he was in any way part of the problem, it was a problem with those individuals and with society at large. Our conversation then deteriorated into a one-way tirade about how I don't know what discrimination truly is, that in Pittsburgh where I come from we have it so good, the culture in and around their town is different than my experiences and a whole lot of other reasons why I just don't get it.

I think that I had said enough and caused enough of a stir for one day so I just listened and let him finish. Understandably, there was a strain on our relationship from that point forward. I realize that what I said may have been difficult to hear and that it was not empathetic but it was the truth as I saw it. He, on the other hand, decided that he would rather not hang out with the guy who is mean and, in his opinion, doesn't really understand advocacy in rural Pennsylvania.

The lesson from this situation is simple. If you are having difficulty in life, sometimes you need to do a self assessment. The problem may not be out there, it might be you.

Think about this

1. Since no one is perfect, how do your imperfections effect those around you?

2. Are there things about yourself that you are unaware of or accept as being you?

3. How will you handle those things moving forward?

http://www.yourmotivationalspeaker.com/still-falling-videos/video19/

Chapter Twenty

Sandy the Social Worker

It has been my privilege to serve on a variety of boards, committees and councils over the last 20 years. Whether it is being the Board President for a local nonprofit or being the chairperson for the PA Statewide Independent Living Council, I am delighted with the opportunity to share my expertise and give back to the community.

One of the times that I look forward to during the committee meetings is the lunch break. There are many reasons for it. First, I like to eat! Second, it's a break from sitting in meetings for what feels like all day. Third, it's a chance to catch up with friends and colleagues. It was during one of those lunch breaks that I had a challenging conversation.

Jim, a friend of mine sat down beside me with a rather disgusted look on his face. I wasn't sure if he had received the wrong meal, was frustrated with what was going on in the meetings or if there was something else going on, so I asked. He shook his head and began to tell me about what was going on with his sister, Sandy.

Sandy is in her mid-30s and has some form of an intellectual disability. She loves people and enjoys going to meetings and events where she can interact with other individuals with disabilities as well as members of the community. My colleague told me that he was becoming frustrated with their local Center for Independent Living. His sister was going to meetings there and, in his words, they were filling her head with garbage.

I wasn't sure exactly what he meant, so I asked for clarification. Jim explained that the staff at the Center for

Independent Living had been talking to Sandy about what she wanted to do with her life. They told her that she could do anything that she wanted to. Apparently, she decided that she wanted to be a social worker. "Imagine," he said, "My sister – a social worker. There's no way!"

He then proceeded to explain to me that Sandy had substantial cognitive limitations. She had received educational services until she was 21 through her local school district and even though she did graduate at the age of 21, she definitely did not function with all of the abilities of the rest of her graduating class. He explained to me how she could not truly live independently. Currently, she was living with her parents and they were talking about what was going to happen with her as they aged. She may be able to move into her own place but she was going to need staff support for any hopes of living independently.

He then began to tell me about how frustrated he was with the staff at the Center for Independent Living. "Why would a fill her head with pipe dreams? Why are they so clueless?" Independent living is a concept that he understands and supports. People with disabilities should live in the community, he said. "I get that." What was frustrating him was the fact that the staff from the Center were so wrapped up in the concept of Independent Living as it is applied generally that they could not see that their ideas were not applicable to his sister in her particular circumstances. "Some people with disabilities are able to live completely on their own and be independent but Sandy is just not one of those people," he stated.

His questions challenged my beliefs about independent living. What he was saying made a lot of sense. It was highly unlikely that his sister would be able to pass the entrance requirements for university enrollment. It was much less likely that she would be able to do any type of graduate level work to get licensure as a social worker. All in all, his assessment was pretty spot on. His sister would likely never be a social worker.

Throughout the afternoon my mind was racing. If Sandy was never going to be a social worker, why would the staff at the Center for Independent living tell her that she could be? Was it a cruel joke? Was it just an overstated belief in the independent living philosophy that she could "do anything she wanted to"?

I looked back at my younger days. As a young child, I wanted to be a superhero. As a teenager, my goal was to play basketball in the NBA. I had to question, how did I do at achieving my goals and was I able to "do anything I wanted to do"? My adult mind quickly told me that I can't do everything that I want. I can't fly and I don't have the ability to become invisible which pretty much rules out my dreams of being a superhero. I have checked my athletic ability as well. I can't shoot a basketball, I can't dribble a basketball, I can't dunk a basketball, I really can't play basketball. So much for my dreams of going to the NBA!

As these realizations settled in, my thoughts started to drift. For my dreams, being a superhero or being in the NBA, why did I want to do those things? As far as being a superhero, there is the prestige of having superpowers but that's not really what I was interested in. Superheroes are people that have taken heroism to the next level. They are not just heroes, they are superheroes. What do heroes do? They help people. Helping people is what I do. That's my job as an advocate for Disability Rights Pennsylvania. I may not be a superhero, but I am hero of sorts. I am helping people who are in difficult circumstances to get out of those circumstances. To be rescued from injustice, oppression and inequality. That sounds kind of like what superheroes do. Except I just do it every day. No superpowers needed, no secret identity, no special superhero costume (thank the Lord that no one has to see me wearing a spandex outfit!).

As far as my dreams about being in the NBA, it broke down into three simple areas. First, it was about basketball, I really like basketball. Second, it was about competition. Last, it was about making money, lots of money! As I look at it, I take each of those on their own to find out whether or not I can accomplish my goals without actually making it to the NBA. At this point in my life, all three of my children are playing basketball. Despite the fact that I can't play, I am heavily involved in the sport. I can talk to them about strategy, give them pointers on how to improve their game and encourage them on how to play the game correctly. I don't have to be in the NBA to be involved in basketball. I don't even have to play myself to be involved. As far as competition goes, there are plenty of places to be involved in competitive activities. Family game night, the office basketball pool (of course only done for bragging rights), you name it. Do I really need to talk about making lots of money? I'm at a point in my life where money is not the most important driving force of my life. It would be nice to have more, but the fact is that I have an amazing wife, three beautiful children, great friends and an awesome extended family. I not sure if more money would truly improve my life but I know this, the more love I have in my life the happier I am!

As I contemplated my dreams and the realization that even though I had not accomplished them as I had originally envisioned, I had actually accomplished everything that I was looking for in those dreams. It was then that I started to dissect my friend's sister's dreams. Did she know what a social worker does on a daily basis? Was she aware of the qualifications for being a social worker? What was a social worker in her world?

I couldn't wait until our dinner break to talk with Jim. As we settled at the table, I told him that I'd been thinking about Sandy's situation all through our afternoon sessions. The fact is that her conundrum had been the only thing on my mind and I missed out on everything we covered in the sessions!

I asked about the role the social worker played in Sandy's life. The social worker helped her interact with the world. When pressed for clarification, Jim told me that the social worker not only setup doctors appointments and therapy visits, the social worker assisted with creating group outings and community involvement. Somewhat out of character (and definitely outside of my comfort zone) I asked how Sandy felt about her social worker (imagine, me asking about feelings!)

As we talked about the social worker, Jim started to focus on what the social worker did, not the peripherals of what a social worker is. In Sandy's world, the social worker was her connection to other people. The social worker made the arrangements for her to get out into the community. Parties and other events at the house were also planned by the social worker. All in all, just about every aspect of Sandy's social interactions was planned by her social worker. (I can't figure out why it took me so long to realize that!)

In that understanding, Sandy could be more involved in planning social activities. She didn't need a license to be able to do that. She didn't need a degree in order to be able to do that. She didn't even need a title to be able to do that. All she needed was an opportunity. Jim looked at me with wide open eyes. He could work with Sandy on these things. Sandy could work with her staff on these things. It was as simple as inviting a friend over for the afternoon. Sandy could work alongside her social worker to determine where her group went for outings. When it came time for her birthday party, Sandy could definitely participate in planning the event. Even if she wasn't a "social worker" she could definitely shape her life experiences as a "social planner".

It's amazing how things begin to open up when you change the way you think! Rather than focusing on what she wants to BE, it's about focusing on what she wants to DO. Sandy's goal was not to actually be a social worker, it was to be more involved in planning social events. In order to facilitate that, the question became, What opportunities does she have to be more involved in the process? What are the steps to get Sandy more involved in creating social experiences?

Think about this
1. What are your goals?
2. What is the difference between want you want to be and what you want to do?
3. What steps do you need to take to reach your goal?

http://www.yourmotivationalspeaker.com/still-falling-videos/video20/

About the Author

Rob Oliver is a speaker, a writer, an advocate, an entrepreneur, a Christian, a husband and a dad. Each of these titles gives an insight into how he thinks, what is important to him and who he truly is.

Speaker: Rob travels the country sharing his message of personal choice, self identity, empowerment and making an impact. His stories resonate with audiences and feedback is highly positive (he has been awarded as the #1 ranked motivational speaker in his home town Pittsburgh market for 2015 and 2016.) With a mixture of humor, passion, emotion and creativity he uses poignant stories to get right to the heart of the essential issues we all share by being human. He enjoys working with meeting planners to ensure that his content meets their outcome expectations for the event and the audience's need. Rob is also a "food guy". One of the things he enjoys most about traveling around is getting recommendations from audience members about the best place in the area to enjoy the area's cuisine.

Writer: His best-selling autobiography, "Still Walking", has been enjoyed by readers around the world. In addition to his own writing, Rob enjoys inspiring young writers during his school visits. He has worked with several other authors to finalize their books and help them navigate the process to get their books published and on the market.

Advocate: Rob's self advocacy started when he was young. As a child he lobbied for the privilege of a later bedtime, the right to have chocolate milk at lunch and the right to ride his sleeping bag down the stairs. The lack of success in his early advocacy (and the reality that riding a sleeping bag down the stairs can be painful) did not deter him. Rob's advocacy has grown from speaking up for his own needs to advocating for others who do not have a strong voice to teaching others how to speak up for themselves. As a result, he has been appointed to the Pennsylvania Community Living Advisory Committee, the Pennsylvania Developmental Disability Council and the Pennsylvania Statewide Independent Living Council where he currently serves as chair.

Entrepreneur: Employment for people with disabilities is a major problem. Rob decided that rather than relying on other people to recognize his strengths and utilize them in their organization, he would use those skills to create his own employment. He has started several small businesses in addition to his speaking and writing work. To him, it's important to provide an example to his children about the power of hard work.

Christian: Rob has a strong faith. Meeting planners can have full confidence that his presentations will be appropriate for any audience. Anyone working with him will attest to the fact that he is honest and a man of his word.

Husband: Becky and Rob have been married since 1994. A marriage of that length requires dedication, flexibility, grace and most of all, love. It's about giving all that you can for the needs of someone else. Rob's dad taught him at a young age that marriage is not a 50/50 relationship, it requires a 100/100 commitment.

Dad: This is Rob's favorite role. In "Still Walking" Rob shared the three things that he is responsible to do as a dad: love his children, teach them right and wrong, and be there for them when they need him. The flexibility of being an entrepreneur allows him to pick them up from practices, eat dinner with them as a family almost every night and be at most of their events and games. Rob works hard to set an example for his kids that there is never a wrong time to do the right thing (or a right time to do the wrong thing.) Food is not just something that Rob enjoys eating, it is also his Love Language. Whenever he is traveling, Rob is always looking for a bakery where he can pick up something sweet to take home to the kids to let them know that are on his heart and mind no matter where he goes.

If you are interested in booking Rob to speak for your organization, please use the booking page on his website (http://www.YourMotivationalSpeaker.com/book-rob.) His site has more information about his presentations as well. You can call him as well at (412) 450-0433. As long as he is not driving, in church, giving a presentation or at one of his kid's games, he will answer directly.

Contact the author:

Rob@YourMotivationalSpeaker.com

(844) ROB-OLIVER

Yes, that number is real.. you can leave off the ER.

(412) 450-0433

Book Rob as a Speaker:

www.yourmotivationalspeaker.com/book-rob

Order Rob's books:

http://www.robsbook.com

Follow Rob on Social Media:

@imroboliver

Instagram twitter Facebook Pinterest